ATTAINING
an ACADEMIC
APPOINTMENT

By

Bill McHenry

S. Kent Butler

Jim McHenry

Atwood Publishing
Madison, WI

Attaining an Academic Appointment
By Bill McHenry, S. Kent Butler, and Jim McHenry

ISBN: 978-1-891859-88-5

© 2012 Atwood Publishing, Madison, WI
www.atwoodpublishing.com

Cover design by TLC Graphics, www.tlcgraphics.com

Library of Congress Cataloging-in-Publication Data
McHenry, Bill, 1971-
Attaining an academic appointment / by Bill McHenry, S. Kent Butler, Jim
McHenry.
p. cm.
Includes bibliographical references and index.
ISBN 978-1-891859-88-5 (pbk.)
1. College teachers—Selection and appointment—United States. 2. College
teachers—Employment—United States. 3. Job hunting—United States. I. Butler,
S. Kent, 1961- II. McHenry, Jim, 1937- III. Title.
LB2332.72.M34 2012
378.1'2—dc23
2012010307

Acknowledgements

BILL MCHENRY: I would like to thank our editorial team for believing in this project, supporting our work, and making the process smooth and professional through every turn. I want to thank my beautiful wife Missy for her encouragement, support, and the kind words she used to help the project continue through each challenging moment. I would like to thank Princess Meghan, Prince Billy, Princess Katie, and Prince Shane for reminding me when I needed to stop writing and start playing. To my wonderful mother Paula I say thank you for all the years of love and support you have given me. Your tireless strength and effort in helping others serves as a beacon when I feel worn down. Without your lessons of perseverance, this book would not be here. I would like to thank my co-authors. Writing with you, Dad, is the most precious piece of my academic life. Thank you Kent for your exceptional word-smithing, powerful writing, and expert knowledge—here's to many years to come. To Lisa and Linda, thanks for continuing to play! Thank you to Kermit and Donna Peters for your loving support, wisdom, and care. Finally, I would like to thank my colleagues and peers for their powerful and meaningful stories. Your nuggets of wisdom and honest truth completed this book.

S. KENT BUTLER: Blessings from above have graced my life with many extraordinary opportunities, much like the opportunity to participate in this particular endeavor. That being said, I would like to thank God for the many gifts he has bestowed upon me. I thank my writing team for inviting me to the table, especially Bill for always keeping us on track throughout the writing process. Gratitude is also extended to our editorial crew for their enthusiastic support of this project. I would also like to express gratitude to my family—Dad, Karen, and Brenda; friends—Cyrus, Tina, Val, Dan, Pat, and Ryan; mentors—Madonna and Tony; and many of my colleagues for their constant encouragement and support. To the narrative contributors—a special thanks to you all for sharing your gifts; your commitment to this project is very much appreciated. Lastly, I want to show gratitude to my strongest supporter, my Mom, who is my constant inspiration. I would like to dedicate this book to her for the love and encouragement I constantly feel shining down upon me every single day.

JIM MCHENRY: I cannot possibly convey the joy I feel in seeing this volume come to fruition. Both Bill and Kent have been excellent collaborators on this project. I also, of course, extend a special thanks to each of the many other contributors to this book: their honesty and candor are both refreshing and illuminating. A special thank you goes out to my friend Dean Stoffer and my former colleague Salene Cower for their ongoing support, and to the Tuesday Morning Regulars who gather each week at the Alfred Stone Center on the Campus of Edinboro University, where the challenging discussions keep all our juices flowing. I thank my wife of forty-five years, Paula, who puts up with me and protects me from interruptions while I'm hacking away on the computer. I am so privileged and blessed to be surrounded by such wonderful people.

Table of Contents

Preface 9

SECTION 1: NUTS AND BOLTS 11

Chapter 1: Introduction 13

Chapter 2: The Position 23

Chapter 3: Your Packet 35

Chapter 4: The Interview Process 55

Chapter 5: The Negotiation 69

SECTION 2: STORIES FROM THE FIELD. 73

Chapter 6: Plan Ahead: Expect the Unexpected 75
    by Jason Willow

Chapter 7: Persistence: Conducting a Successful Search
    in a Tough Market 85
    by Bradley Will

Chapter 8: The Old Dog Learns a New Trick: Academia's
    Research-Faculty Track 89
    by Darin J. Knapp

Chapter 9: A Single Parent's Perspective 95
    by Susan L. Hegel

Chapter 10: Finding my Place. 99
    by Jill M. Schultz

Chapter 11: The On-Campus Interview in the Academic
 Search Process: A Retrospective View 103
 by Frank Main

Chapter 12: The Academic Job Search as an Exciting Time: Taking
 Pragmatic Steps to Land a Position in Higher Education 109
 by Jim Saiers

Chapter 13: Finding the Right Faculty Position:
 The Importance of Fit. 115
 by Jim Machell

Chapter 14: Interview Process and Candidate Selection
 for an Academic Position in Chemistry. 123
 by James D. Hoefelmeyer

Chapter 15: From Professional to Professor: Reflections
 on Mid-career Entry into Higher Education 133
 by Phillip F. Diller

Chapter 16: De-emphasizing Goodness-of-Fit in the Hiring Process:
 What Can We Learn from Adoptive Family Adjustment?. 137
 by Steve Saiz

Chapter 17: Finding the Fit: The Minutiae of the Academic
 Job Search 145
 by Amie A. Doughty

Chapter 18: Life is a Journey, Not a Destination:
 Trust your Board of Directors 153
 by Darren E. Dobrinski

Chapter 19: Pay Attention to the Details 159
 by Matt Walker

Chapter 20: Do What You Love 169
 by Richard L. Schwab

Chapter 21: Interviewing For Positions in Higher Education:
 Lessons Learned 181
 by Janelle Cowles

Chapter 22: Are You Taking Care of Those Closest to You
    During the Search?. 187
  by Linda McHenry

APPENDICES 193

List of annotated references and useful resources
    for the job searcher 207

Index. 211

About the Authors 215

Preface

Welcome to our book, which will guide you through the process of searching for a job in academia. For each of us, sharing our knowledge and personal experiences of this critical time in an academic's life has been rewarding; what we offer is a set of strategies and body of advice that will help you find the right fit in the academy: the right institution, the right department, and the right colleagues. During our own job searches, we all benefitted from supportive people and abundant words of wisdom, but felt the need for a book that would tell us what to expect of the process as a whole: the opportunities, and how to use them; the roadblocks, and how to cope with them. Each of us found a place in academia at the end of a unique journey, and we trust that this book will assist you during yours.

The book contains two main parts: Section 1 details the stages of the job search and provides practical techniques for navigating them. Section 2 features personal narratives written by a diverse sample of current academic faculty. These rich and engaging reflections describe the sometimes daunting, sometimes grueling dimensions of even those searches that end in success.

INVITATION TO READERS

Our aim in writing this book was to help academics transition from their current positions (as doctoral students or faculty members) to other fulfilling places in the academic world. As with all books, we wrote, rewrote, discussed, checked our spelling, got to a certain point, sent it to the publisher. . .and the result rests in your hands. We're not sure we're done—we actually see this as a first effort. There are many more stories out there that could deepen this project.

So if you wish, it's your turn: we invite you to author your own story. What was your particular job search like?

We promise to carefully read every submission, and if there is a second edition of this book, we will consider your material for publication. To share your story, send it to:

Bill McHenry
UC 200
Texas A&M University-Texarkana
7101 University Ave
Texarkana, Texas 75505

SECTION 1

The Nuts and Bolts

CHAPTER I

Introduction

The fundamental rock on which this book is anchored is that many of the most important aspects of the job search are either completely or partially *under your control*. It follows that, since you actually control the process, you are also almost completely responsible for it. Therefore, you should recognize that your job search is where you really begin to define yourself as a professional and build the launching pad for your career. Of course, you will also need to remember that there are times when you have no real control. For example, while all job postings bear the trappings of being open to any fully-qualified applicant, and are replete with legally required statements of fairness, we all know that some positions were penciled in for someone's brother-in-law before the ink was dry on the original advertisement. However, we think this state of affairs is less common today.

It's no overstatement to say that you are poised at one of the major turning points in academic life. Your immediate task is to begin orchestrating a transition from your recent (successful) role as a matriculating doctoral student or faculty member at Institution A to that of a clearly recognized, professional tenure-track instructor (or, even better, assistant professor) at Institution B. The diligence, effort, and skill you bring to bear in this transformation will have major ramifications for your long-term success as a professional and, probably, your overall degree of personal satisfaction.

Of course, going from Institution A to a new role at Institution B means making a choice. There are many institutions of higher education in the United States: B is only one of them. You will have to decide to place yourself there. For comparison, recall that you probably considered several institutions when you resolved to start your doctoral studies, then winnowed the list to the one you chose—and, importantly, the one that chose you.

We'd like you to read the following questions, then close the book. After closing the book, use the questions to reflect quietly and calmly on just how you want to spend the next period of your life. (Of course, the list we've compiled is far from comprehensive, and you will need to prioritize your own set of "absolute musts," "nice to haves," "very desirables," "fine if they're there," and "no big deal to me." No one else can do this for you.)

- What kind of position are you seeking?
- Do you want to be at a major research university?
- Do you want to be at a college that places highest priority (and rewards) on classroom teaching performance?
- Do you want to be at a small school, a large school, or somewhere in the middle?
- Do you want to be in a place where research and publishing is prized?
- Do you want to be near a coastline?
- Do you want to be in a big city? A small town?
- What salary do you need? What benefit package?
- What size department do you want to work in?
- How important is the accreditation status of the university or department?
- How important are duties like advising, conference presentations, and community service?
- What types of faculty support would you like to have?

Keep in mind that embarking on the job-search process puts you at the mercy of some variables that you cannot control; you may not be able to find a position that's ideal for you in every way, but that doesn't necessarily speak to an inadequacy on your part. After all, when Albert Einstein—arguably the single greatest mind of the twentieth century—completed his studies, he wasn't able to find an academic post anywhere, and ended up working in the patent office.

Having identified at least some of your preferences, you probably also have some feel for the task ahead. The authors and individual contributors to this volume will flesh out that feeling by sharing some of the hills and valleys, the highs and lows, and the successes and failures they experienced as they traveled (travailed) the path on which you find yourself. They've been as forthright as possible in sharing the unique and personal adventures of their searches; in addition, their testimonies are shaped by valuable experiences on the other side of the process, since many of them have seen extensive service as members of search committees.

Prior to launching into the mechanics of your job search, we'll take a moment to highlight something that's often ignored or given insufficient consideration: the emotional costs of this endeavor.

Imagine hearing on Monday about a position that would be perfect for you. Let's say it's at a university twenty minutes from your home, has all the benefits you desire, and fits your particular professional qualifications to a T. You're as excited and charged as you get—primed to go, filled with energy. You gather your application materials and send them to the committee by Thursday. You then begin to daydream about the position. Positives abound.

And yet, as the weeks go by, your enthusiasm is replaced by other emotions, ranging from a more realistic, subdued excitement on the positive side all the way to fear and a creeping despair on the negative. You begin to wonder: "What if I don't get an interview? What if they interview me, and I bomb? What if I get the job and it's not right for me?"

The internal questions go on and on.

The application deadline passes. You hear nothing. Another week goes by, then still another. Gradually, your second-guessing shifts from your behavior to theirs: "What's wrong with those people? Why haven't they contacted me? Do I really want to work with people who are so inconsiderate?"

A month or so after the deadline, you've received nothing but a form letter indicating that your materials arrived. You're angry at them for not contacting you. Simultaneously, you're upset with yourself for "not being good enough," or "not having done enough," or "not having done a better job on your cover letter or your vitae" . . . and on and on. Your self-statements now start with "I should have . . . !" or "Why didn't I . . .?"

Unfortunately, this scenario is not uncommon in the academic world. During your search, you (and those close to you) may experience extreme emotional pushes and pulls, jarring ups and downs, tremendous stresses —all of which are part of the rewarding, unpredictable, bruising, and elevating (pick any of these descriptors, or add your own) road to success.

A key insight that's always difficult to swallow is that sometimes the best candidate (who may in fact be you) is simply not chosen. When this occurs, it is very painful. (It's also counterproductive, for when the candidate selected is less qualified, the institution often finds itself conducting another costly search to fill the same position.)

So, adding to our previous scenario, imagine discovering that the position you wanted has been accepted by a former colleague, a friend who matriculated in the same doctoral program as you. You know the good, the bad, and the ugly about this person; you clearly (let's allow, accurately) judge him or her to possess less ability than you when it comes to the qualifications for this job. The entire hiring process might begin to take on a somewhat surreal feeling, causing you to wonder "What does he or she have that I don't?" or "I remember he or she barely made it through our first semester. How could he or she have been chosen over me!" The important point here is that, given the imperfections inherent in the search process, you often pay a heavy psychological price when competing with candidates you actually know.

Another major stressor, already noted above, is that you may have to wait a long time before you receive any sort of meaningful reply from the institution. Your authors can attest that some universities do not appear to have effective procedures in place to verify receipt of your materials. Even those that do provide such notification may not contact you again for many months—in some cases, ever.

We've emphasized these taxing factors because it's important for you to recognize, early in the process, the need to draw on whatever strategies have enabled you to deal with stress and uncertainty in the past. It may be helpful to try to see the process from the other side. Remind yourself, for instance, that ethical search committees will want to take the time needed to make the right decisions regarding applicants. From your viewpoint, these committees may move agonizingly slowly, but keep in mind that the task of serving on search committees is simply added to faculty members' regular duties; it's an additional task that may be difficult to work into each committee member's schedule.

Thus, potential vexations exist on both ends. What's important is for you to choose to be as proactive as possible. During a period of waiting, work on things like preparing some of your dissertation material for publication, writing a proposal for one of your professional conferences, or systematically collecting as much information as possible about the universities to which you've applied.

Surprisingly, an agonizing waiting period often ends in an abrupt flurry of action. You might receive many phone calls and have your candidacy investigated by a committee member—or even several different committees—over a relatively short period of time. After not hearing a word for two months, you could receive calls from two different committees in a single day. The next day could bring a response from a third institution. Later in the week, a fourth school might log in. At such a point, having gone from feeling like you have no options to feeling overwhelmed by their sheer number, you will have to 1) understand that you might not be able to attend interviews at all the schools, and 2) make some very significant personal choices very quickly. As we'll discuss in Chapter 3, thorough research on the variables of each position, department, and university will assist you immensely in making solid choices.

Your options might be imperfect. For example, if several different institutions want you to visit their campuses and go through the campus selection process, you might need to turn down a school that seemed promising. In terms of logistics, understand that each visit is likely to consume two days, and every one of the several universities in play may want to get you through the process within the next two or three weeks—after all, they have various (now suddenly pressing) deadlines to meet. You also may have time commitments that you cannot break or modify. Decisions will have to be made regarding which invitations to accept and which to decline. These decisions are usually irrevocable. By choosing to visit institution A and not institution B, you will select one path and close off the other.

Patience, uncertainty, decisions . . . this process is not for the faint-hearted or the unprepared. Knowing this, we strongly suggest that you take pragmatic steps to increase your effectiveness: exercise regularly, practice relaxation techniques, share personal concerns with willing and active listeners, and remember to reserve some time for getting completely away from your job search. This allows you to re-energize yourself and deepen your perspective.

WHERE TO START

One excellent starting point is the recognition that, being proficient in academics, you are capable of obtaining and managing a lot of information. Information will provide you with a base. As you go along, your creativity will also be extremely important, but for starters, you'll need to garner some "stuff." All of us—Einstein with physics, Mozart with music, and a child learning her ABC's—need a certain amount of information before we can become creatively and effectively self-directed. In other words, you have to know some things before you can discover something.

So what are your best sources of information? At first, they'll probably be some combination of the following: your major advisor, key professors in your department, your dissertation chair/others on your committee, and any other people in your area of expertise with whom you've developed professional and/or personal relationships. In completing your work at the university, and through your experiences in internships, practica, and the like, you have certainly rubbed shoulders with many professionals in your field. These individuals know both you and a lot of what is really going on in your field (professionals in almost any field are a subset of a subset of society). They are often aware of existing position announcements and, sometimes even more importantly, positions that may be opening in the near future, parallel to your job-search window. And of course, these professionals will prove invaluable in your networking.

Having noted all that, the truth remains that your professional colleagues can't find and secure a position for you. That responsibility lies with you, and you *do* have the skill and talent that it demands. Completing the classwork and dissertation leading to your terminal degree is an absolute testimony to your organizational skills. You can do this. It will simply take focused and dedicated effort.

TIME

As you embark on your endeavor, it's important to consider the amount of time involved in the steps we're laying out (e.g., putting together paper credentials, establishing campus contacts, and completing interviews). It might be useful to compare this process to buying a car. We all know it's only a *suggestion*, in the newspaper advertisement, that a particular car will cost $14,999 (advertised, of course, as "under $15,000"). You can be fairly certain that when the final numbers are tallied, you'll be spending more —think closer to $17-18,000, or, if you really get carried away, $20,000+. Similarly, the amount of time you'll need to carry your search to its successful conclusion is likely to be more than you first expect; to wit, some of us are still working on paying back the $20,000 we spent on our under-$15,000 cars.

For the moment, let's look at just one example. One of the earliest tasks in your campaign should be the construction of at least a skeletal version of your vitae. Later in the process, each set of credentials you submit will need to be tailored to the specific position for which you're applying. If Position A is heavily weighted toward candidates with an affinity for conducting research, then your paper credentials need to highlight your research achievements. Conversely, if the requirements for Position B emphasize classroom teaching abilities, your credentials will need to do the same. (We should note here that you must *not* put anything in your credentials that isn't true.) It is not wise to be coy and modest at this point. If you have the skills needed for the position, be sure to let the committee know it. Do not assume they'll be able to read between the lines.

All of this refining and re-authoring takes time, energy, and effort. So how do you do it? How do you begin?

Well, for starters, pick up your personal calendar and mark the date on which you'll finish your preliminary (skeletal) vitae. Then set target dates for completing:

1. A list of features that you want or need in an academic position

2. A list of assets and strengths you will try to bring to any position

3. A list, with associated bookmarks, of the websites that advertise jobs in your discipline

4. A rough draft of your cover letter

With these steps, you will move forward proactively. The more time and quality effort you expend now, the easier and more productive the process will become.

DIVERSITY

On many college campuses, diversity is an important factor in the hiring of new faculty. Most search committees require paperwork and certain steps in the process to ensure that diverse populations are both encouraged to apply and given equal consideration. Committees may (this is not an absolute rule) have a strong desire to fill a vacancy with a member of an underrepresented demographic group. Fair or not, this is a reality of some searches. On the other hand, homophobia, racism, sexism, and various other noxious "isms" persist in academia—naturally, their magnitudes vary from institution to institution.

We can't tell you whether to disclose your race, ethnicity, disability, religious beliefs, etc., but we do suggest that you consider carefully the degree to which you want to reveal your true self, especially early in the process. It's hard to tell whether it will help, hurt, or leave unaffected your chance of being invited for an interview. For instance, one of the authors was interviewed at a university where he really wanted to work. Things went very well, and he got excellent vibes about his prospects. Yet toward the end of the second day, the committee chair—who'd said earlier, "You are our guy"—pulled him aside and said, "I could be fired for this, but I want to be straight with you: the committee has decided that we need to hire a woman. I'm sorry." This example is somewhat unique, what with the chair being so forthright, but it highlights the fact that, in some cases, your being hired hinges on aspects of your identity that you cannot change.

In assembling this book, we paid special attention to inviting diverse voices for

NOTE:

One of the authors was asked to present at a regional conference. The presentation was composed of five diverse faculty members from across the country, who discussed issues of diversity related to teaching. Not all of the presenters had met prior to the conference. In fact, for some, their first interactions occurred five minutes before the presentation.

During the course of the presentation, one of the presenters (who belonged to a minority group) happened to point toward someone he'd not previously met. He said something like, "because Joe is White . . ." With a comforting smile, Joe replied, "You're making a big assumption when you call me White . . .". Immediately, the presenter realized the mistake; the two professionals then created a wonderful learning/teaching moment as they processed the ramifications of the erroneous ethnic label.

the chapters. Though we could not, of course, represent every minority group, you will read authors who are African American, Native American, White, Latino, members of the Gay/Lesbian/Bi-Sexual/Trans-Gendered (GLBT) community, and persons with disabilities. Moreover, because diversity can be understood in terms of different disciplines, geographic locations, institutional settings (urban, suburban, rural), and institutional sizes, we have attempted to include diverse voices in these areas, too. You will read the experiences of faculty members serving in Carnegie I institutions, large metropolitan schools, smaller rural colleges, and community colleges. Numerous disciplines are represented. The mix is further broadened by the inclusion of both younger and more seasoned perspectives.

Differences in applicants based on race, ethnicity, disability, sexual orientation, gender, and the like may or may not be apparent to search-committee members through written credentials or even on-campus presentations. It is always a judgment call as to if or when such information should be forwarded.

HOW WE ORGANIZED THIS BOOK

The following chapters (Chapter 2-5) discuss distinct aspects of the academic job search. Though written as separate entities, the elements they describe are thoroughly intertwined.

Chapter 2 covers how to assess the parameters of a position, including analysis of the position announcement and factors to consider during the application and interview stages. One major goal here is to identify the announcements that appeal to you most, which involves systematically judging the fit between you and the positions described. Effort expended here will save time and resources by enabling you to focus more clearly on positions suited to your talents.

Chapter 3 covers the materials included in your application packet. Though some disciplines feature unique materials, this section covers the standard fare. Also offered here are guidelines for the creation of a cover letter and vitae.

Chapter 4 explains some of the mechanics of search committees. Although the nature of the search process dictates that every committee is different, they do tend to share certain characteristics and patterns. The chapter also contains a discussion of practical considerations pertaining to both campus and phone interviews.

Chapter 5 provides some tips for developing the best possible contract once you have been selected for a position.

These four "how you might do it" chapters are followed by chapters written by current faculty members and administrators who have been on both sides of the academic job search. Their testimonials contain excellent counsel, even when they describe false starts. They are often shot through with strong emotion, and while real pain and disappointment are occasionally evident, so are enthusiasm and fulfillment. We place a high value on the sharing contained in these pieces; we not only hope, but believe that they will help you succeed in your own job search.

CHAPTER 2

The Position

Virtually every academic position is unique. Therefore, a "one size fits all" campaign simply will not work. Firing off resumes in all directions, coupled with bland "touch all bases" cover letters, costs time and money but is not likely to bear fruit. A much more promising and proactive method is to tailor each of your applications as specifically as possible to the requirements of the position. Depending on your discipline, there may be dozens and dozens of job postings to review (as in psychology), or only a handful (as in actuary science). Whatever the case, one of your initial tasks is to sort through various lists of openings and identify those positions best suited to your talents and preferences.

WHERE TO LOOK

There are many sources of accurate and timely information on open positions. As mentioned in Chapter 1, your academic contacts (professors, former /present colleagues, friends in the field) may have information regarding both current and anticipated possibilities. Consulting these experts represents a crucial, regular job-seeking task.

Numerous websites are dedicated to academic job listings. General sites, such as HigherEdJobs.com and chroniclecareers.com, offer listings in many fields. These are very useful, but you will also need to search websites dedicated specifically to your discipline, as well as your national and regional/state organizations. Once you have located these sources, you should bookmark them and check them on a regular basis. Additionally, you should take a look at the websites of universities that appeal to you, as these will often provide lists and descriptions of openings.

So, keep in mind that there are many sources for you to tap in this quest. Also keep in mind that you need to remain diligent and consistent, which means developing a regular pattern of checking and rechecking possible sources, even though there may be weeks, perhaps months, when nothing of real interest surfaces —nothing that suits your specialty or your pocketbook. This, too, is part of the process, and you may rest assured that persistence will eventually be rewarded. Inactivity and/or irregularity will not. (See Table 1.)

TYPE OF POSITION

Many universities will only accept application materials submitted for specific positions; they will not hold your materials for positions which might open in the future. Submission of materials for non-existent positions is therefore really wasteful.

Printed advertisements (found in professional journals and newsletters) list positions that may or may not be advertised on internet sites. In some cases, these sources may elaborate on web-based advertisements.

A college professor is not a college professor is not a college professor. That is, different universities place different priorities on their professors' major duties: classroom teaching, research/publication (scholarship), and service to the university/community/discipline. For example, required teaching loads may range from a high of four or five courses per semester to a low of, believe it or not, no courses whatsoever. There is generally an inverse relationship between hours devoted to the classroom and hours devoted to leading or coordinating research- or grant-writing. Academic positions that require teaching loads of fifteen credit-hours per semester may require little or no research/publication, while others may require faculty members to teach only one class per semester but expect (read: require) them to publish

MEDIUM	SOURCE	DAILY	WEEKLY	BI-MONTHLY	MONTHLY
Internet	HigherEdJobs.com	X			
	chroniclecareers.com	X			
	listserves	X			
Journals	(e.g., Hispanic Today)				X
Professors	(e.g., Dr. Smith)			X	
Friends	(e.g., Paul Jones)			X	

Table 1: Guide to where to look

several articles per year in nationally-refereed journals. Such dramatic differences may be present not only between universities, but between the various colleges of a single university and even between programs housed in a single college.

Many universities expect a minimum of two or three professional publications prior to any faculty member being considered for promotion, as from assistant professor to associate professor. (From top to bottom, the academic ranks are: professor, associate professor, assistant professor, and instructor.) Acceptable articles may be published in either state or national journals. Certain universities might require that you publish one or more articles per year in national journals.

At some universities and within some departments, grant-writing is optional: you may seek grant-based funding if you wish, but it is not required for promotion or tenure. At other universities, a faculty member's role may center almost exclusively on acquiring and implementing grants.

Virtually all academic positions require some measure of service to the university. This requirement is often met within your department, program area, or college division; it may also fall into a university-wide group. Additionally, you might be expected to serve on state-wide committees within your curriculum, or to provide committee service to your profession through state, regional, and/or national organizations.

Presentations at local, state, regional, and/or national conferences may also be required as a part of the promotion and tenure process. In fact, in some departments, these activities are a part of the norm (i.e., several faculty get together and present at their regional or state conference each year). (See Table 2, which shows the variability of positions.)

PAY

The financial aspects of a position are, of course, a major consideration. There is a wide range of salaries available for academic faculty, and those salaries are affected by many variables. For example, a salary may be influenced by the geographic location of the university in question, or by whether the school is public or private. Such factors are not often absolute, and a department may be able to offer a higher starting salary based on its unique (possibly urgent) needs, its current enrollment, the financial stability of the university, additional funding sources, or the particular specialty you have.

	SCHOOL A	SCHOOL B	SCHOOL C	SCHOOL D	SCHOOL E
Teaching*	7	3	5	I	7
Notes	4 classes/ semester	2 classes/ semester	3 classes/ semester	I-2 classes/ year	3 classes fall, 4 spring: a lot of interest in evaluations
Scholarly Activities*	I	5	5	7	4
Notes	I-2 articles in first 5 years in state journals	I article in national peer-reviewed journals per year	I article in national peer-reviewed journals per year	I-2 articles in national peer-reviewed journals per year	3-4 articles in first 5 years in state journals
Service*	4	4	4	I	2
Notes	Several committees (university-wide, college, & department)	Several committees (university-wide, college, & department)	Several committees (university-wide, college, & department)	No required committee or service work	Little to no committee work required
Grants*	I	I	4	7	2
Notes	No grant-writing	No grant-writing	Some involvement in collaborative grant-writing	Required to secure external funds to cover cost of position	Involvement in grant-writing only if interested

*Scale: I—lowest weight (e.g., teaching 0-I courses/semester); 7—highest weight (e.g., 4 courses/ semester + heavy weight on student evaluations)

Table 2: Guide to the type of position

Conversely, at some universities, pay for a given rank may be relatively non-negotiable. This is often the result of collective bargaining agreements or university policies. However, even in these instances, you may be able to negotiate regarding your entry rank. It is important to recognize that increasing your starting level by even one step can have a dramatic effect on your total remuneration over your career.

When it comes to judging salary offers, you may be able to establish general parameters by checking with people in your discipline as to the typical range their universities offer to someone in your field, at your rank. Expect to encounter discrepancies of $5,000 to $15,000, or even greater, and be careful not to automatically value too highly the university with the highest starting pay. Other remuneration factors can strongly affect this raw number. Perhaps at the university that offers $7,000 more per year, you are required to pay $600 per month for family health care coverage, while at the second university, your medical insurance is only $65 per month. Suddenly, that $7,000 advantage has decreased to $580 for the year. Now let's say the first university has you paying $25 per month for parking, while at the second, parking is free. The original $7,000 is reduced by another $300 per year. And don't forget to compare the cost of living between the two university communities.

BENEFITS

The costs of health care, retirement planning, and overall benefit plans differ significantly from school to school. With this in mind, you will need to consider both your current and projected needs as a preliminary step in your job search. As with pay differences, benefit plans should be reviewed as *total packages*, as opposed to simply isolating only one or two factors. The following example of a checklist should help you start your evaluation of the benefits of various programs; naturally, your specific needs and life-style will help you rank-order the list. (See Table 3 and also Appendix C for a reproducible copy of this guide.)

OTHER BENEFITS

Ancillary benefits may include such items as parking rates, the cost of attending sporting events, and day care and dining facilities. Table 4 offers a guide that will help you organize these benefits for comparison.

No matter what you decide regarding your needs in terms of salary and benefits, you must choose between working at a school that has an organized group in charge of negotiating future pay raises and benefits, and a university that allows the administration to make such decisions unilaterally. Schools in the former category seem to have fewer changes in benefits from year to year, while those in the latter may be subject to change more frequently from one year to another.

LOCATION

When conducting a national search, your field of vision may cover schools in rural, suburban, and urban areas. Although you may initially feel that all

SCHOOL		UNIVERSITY A	UNIVERSITY B
School Unionized (Y/N)		Yes	No
Cost of medical coverage		$100/month	$450/month
	Dependents covered (Y/N)	Yes	No
	Major medical (Y/N)	Yes	No
	Co-pay for doctor	$10	$20
	Deductible	$125/person	$200
	Notes	PPO: Well-baby care	HMO
Cost of prescriptions		0	0
	Co-pay/ prescription	$10/15	$20/25
	Deductible	$100	$150
Cost of dental		0	$150
	Dependents covered (Y/N)	Y	N
	Notes	$75/person/year	$50/person/year
Cost of vision		0	$12/month
	Dependents covered (Y/N)	Yes	Yes
	Notes	$75 every 2 years	$100 every 2 years

Table 3: Guide to benefits

areas are acceptable, you would be wise to spend some time seriously considering this variable, as it affects such things as cost of living, commute durations, and the type of activities available in the area (e.g., recreation, churches, public schools, etc.).

Along these same lines, your search should probably be targeted on those parts of the country where you'd like to settle for the long haul. If you were born and reared in the Midwest and have strong family roots there, a position on the coast might not be a good fit; the move might be alluring, but understand that when you apply for a position, your employer, colleagues, and students expect you to hold it for more than a few years.

SCHOOL	UNIVERSITY A	UNIVERSITY B
Parking	$25/month	$1/semester
Sporting events	$4-15/event	Free
Concerts and plays	Free	$5-8/event
Child care	Not available	$375/month full-time
Dining	$4/lunch	$6-7/lunch

Table 4: Guide to ancillary benefits

In sum, when you consider your dream job, think a while about where you see yourself now and for some time to come. Table 5 will aid you in identifying significant differences between locations from your personal point of view.

SIZE OF DEPARTMENT / PROGRAM

Careful consideration should be given to the size of the "nuclear" group of people with whom you will be working. All departments have issues, concerns, systemic problems, and the like. Your personality, previous work experiences, and personal needs probably suggest whether you are likely to be more effective in a small, medium, or large department.

The size of the department you work in may also be directly related to things like resources, allocations, power and promotion, and tenure. A small program might be appealing if you feel it will help you develop personal relationships with your colleagues, but the program's resources may

SCHOOL	UNIVERSITY A	UNIVERSITY B
Geographic location	East Coast	Midwest
Urban, suburban, rural	Urban	Rural
Cost of living	High	Medium
Commute time	45-60 minutes	5-10 minutes
Distance to family	20 hours	3 hours
Area activities	Big city, pro sports, many churches, hurricane area	Camping, hiking, small community

Table 5: Guide to location

be relatively limited. The needs of a larger program can come across as more compelling, especially since its size increases the volume of its collective voice. This is not to say that a department's or program's size always correlates to resource allocation—it's simply a good thing to keep in mind.

ACCREDITATION

Consideration should be given to the professional accreditations of not only the department, but also the college and university. Program accreditations indicate at least minimal levels of professional affiliation and suggest that appropriate allocations of resources are being made to meet specific professional standards. Furthermore, accreditations often signal an institutional commitment to growth and continued refinement of both specific programs and the greater university. Lack of such distinctions is a red flag that bears at least an inquiry. Since universities, colleges, and departments are (or at least should be) dynamic and forward looking, noting whether they are moving toward either attaining or retaining accreditation is important to you as a potential faculty member. (See Table 6.)

RESPONSIBILITIES

Every hiring committee will size you up in many ways. Its members will be envisioning you as a potential colleague and considering which of the department's needs will be met by your specific skill set: "What can this person be expected to do?" While you may be applying for a "teaching position," other responsibilities may be being penciled in as givens. Unless you ask, to your dismay, you may not discover those responsibilities until sometime later. For example, perhaps you've indicated on your vitae that you did some work on your doctoral program's accreditation efforts. Seeing this, the committee may project you into the lead position of its upcoming attempt at re-accreditation. Unless you ask *during the search/match process* about activities that the department might want you to undertake, you will not be fully aware of its plans for you. So use any available opening to get a feel for how the department operates—how its work gets done. Remember: the fewer surprises, the better.

TECHNOLOGY

Technology has long been spreading across the landscape of academia, and there's no end in sight. The current generation and all that follow must be

	UNIVERSITY-WIDE (E.G., MIDDLE STATES)		COLLEGE (E.G., NCATE)		DEPARTMENT (E.G., APA)	
University A	Yes	No	Yes	No	Yes	No
University B	Yes	No	Yes	No	Yes	No
University C	Yes	No	Yes	No	Yes	No
University D	Yes	No	Yes	No	Yes	No
University E	Yes	No	Yes	No	Yes	No
University F	Yes	No	Yes	No	Yes	No
University G	Yes	No	Yes	No	Yes	No

Table 6: Guide to accreditation

capable of utilizing increasingly complex and sophisticated tools. From distance education to streaming video used both synchronously and asynchronously, classroom technology continues to grow in both use and utility. You should pay attention to how each of the schools on your list incorporates and adapts to technological developments.

Part of this, of course, is assessing the fit between your teaching style and the technologies available on campus. If your style of instruction requires certain technologies, it's important to find out whether they are available within the department you're considering. For example, if you teach using BlackBoard (an online adjunct platform used to either augment or completely house course information, such as syllabi, examinations, slide shows, and data sets) or PowerPoint presentations and find that the department has no interest in such methods, you must factor that stance into your deliberation. In a similar vein, if you apply for a position that uses distance education almost exclusively to reach students, but you prefer to work almost exclusively within a typical physical classroom, the fit may not be very good. (See Table 7.)

ORIGINS OF THE OPENING

Early in the process, you should try to ascertain the origins of the job opening in which you're interested. A position usually opens for specific reasons. It may be a replacement for a retiring faculty member, or for one who has moved to either another university or another position within the same university. The department might need to create a new position because of increased enrollment or because it wants to start a new program (e.g., rehabilitation counseling in a counseling department that does not offer that specialty). Investigating how an opening emerged may lead you to discover, for example, that particular departments have openings year after year. Annual searches may simply suggest that the department is experiencing a time of transition, with many older faculty seeking retirement.

FINANCIAL POSITION OF THE UNIVERSITY

The shifting sands of the university landscape can be difficult to read. Predicting the financial position of a particular institution ten years down the road (with the possible exception of the Yales and Harvards) rarely yields any kind of certainty. Nevertheless, it is clearly in your best interest to find out as much as you can about the fiscal health of the universities to

	DISTANCE EDUCATION (e.g., video-conferencing technologies for the classroom)		COURSE AUGMENTATION TECHNOLGIES (e.g., BlackBoard)		CLASSROOM TECHNOLOGIES (e.g., computers in the classroom, smart carts, video-projectors)	
University A	Yes	No	Yes	No	Yes	No
Notes						
University B	Yes	No	Yes	No	Yes	No
Notes						
University C	Yes	No	Yes	No	Yes	No
Notes						
University D	Yes	No	Yes	No	Yes	No
Notes						
University E	Yes	No	Yes	No	Yes	No
Notes						
University F	Yes	No	Yes	No	Yes	No
Notes						

Table 7: Guide to technology

which you are applying. Sources of this information may include people with whom you interview, former employees of the school in question, colleagues in the field, local newspapers, and the university website.

The financial position of a university has a major impact on the atmosphere and attitude of the faculty, administration, staff, and students. Furthermore, if a university without a collective-bargaining agreement or union runs into financial trouble (perhaps the state has cut some of its funding), the salaries and benefits of faculty and staff will almost inevitably suffer. Raises that were discussed or even promised will either evaporate quickly or amount to much less than anticipated. (See Table 8.)

NOTE:

Sometimes a pension window (a strategic financial maneuver used to recalibrate salaries that allows individuals who are close to retirement to retire at a higher rate than they might otherwise) will open, often for a limited period of time, which will "shake the trees."

More ominously, such churning could also indicate a difficult work environment in which faculty members (especially younger faculty members) with options tend to vote with their feet: they quickly utilize opportunities to relocate. The truth is that openings can come about for any number of reasons: a thriving department, maybe, or a need to balance the student/faculty ratio. As a job seeker, it's best for you to know.

FUNDING FOR CONFERENCES, LICENSES, CERTIFICATIONS, AND PROFESSIONAL ORGANIZATIONS

Like everything else—electricity, a good cup of coffee, a gallon of gas—the costs associated with maintaining professional standing through attendance at conferences and licensure/certification within your discipline will continue to increase.

Since you may have to spend several thousand dollars a year on this type of thing, knowing the policies

NOTE:

Please remember that if you hold student membership in any professional organization in your field, you will discover upon the renewal date that you are now eligible to pay the regular fee, which, naturally, is higher.

33

SCHOOL	UNIVERSITY A	UNIVERSITY B
Size of department	3	12
Responsibilities	Accreditation report	Develop clinic
Position I am filling	Replacing faculty who was there 1 year	New position, growth
Financial position of university	Stagnant	Growing rapidly
Funding for conferences, etc.	$500/year	$2,000/year

Table 8: Guide to ancillary department/university issues

of your targeted university, school, and department is important, both professionally and fiscally. For example, if the university expects you to regularly attend and present at national conferences, and to maintain credentials (i.e., professional license/certification), but provides little or no provision for helping you with the corresponding costs, you'd rather know about it *before* accepting a contract.

CHAPTER 3

Your Packet

Meeting a search committee in person (either at the airport or during a first tour of the campus) does not, of course, represent the first opportunity this group has had to form significant—possibly various—opinions about you. That initial contact took place when the committee reviewed your application materials, or packet (usually done individually by each member and, later, as a group). First impressions of you may have been favorable (likely) or unfavorable, and probably evolved somewhat through follow-ups with your listed recommenders.

A search that ends with an offer of employment from your target institution relies largely on the use of known strategies, and meticulously tailoring your entire application packet to the exact position requirements is one of the most important, an absolute necessity. Keep in mind that your goal in this early stage is not to secure the position, but to receive an invitation to interview for the position. Because the committee may be required to cull dozens of packets, yours must catch some attention, must sparkle. Those that present a "Dear Occupant" flavor simply won't survive the first round.

There are several tasks for you to work on even before you zero in on the universities that best fit your career plans. You should get your letters of recommendation in order. You should copy and organize your teaching artifacts. You should organize your professional writing, your professional presentations, and your service-oriented activities.

LETTERS OF RECOMMENDATION

Months before you plan to begin submitting applications, you will need to request that several significant professionals in your network write letters of recommendation on your behalf. The people you ask must be able to positively and effectively address your personal and professional strengths.

Good timing is crucial, here. Any faculty member who's served more than a semester or two has met the well-meaning student who bursts into the office in desperate need of a letter of recommendation (which should actually have been completed last Thursday) so he or she can apply for the position of his or her dreams. That professors have a) final examinations to administer/score, b) final grades to calculate, c) daunting piles of final papers to read and evaluate, and d) several committee meetings to chair or attend—these things strike the student as immaterial. Is it any wonder, then, that many letters of recommendation do so little to positively sway search committees? Semesters have fairly predictable life cycles, and picking a quieter time might result in a faster turnaround and, more significantly, a better letter. When your recommenders have time to really reflect on you, they may actually craft material with some sparkle, the kind that makes a search committee sit up and take notice.

You will usually need to have at least three letters forwarded in support of your other written credentials; occasionally, as many as six or seven will be required. Choose your recommenders carefully. Make sure to ask good writers who are in good standing in the discipline, since every letter reflects on you through more than its expressed content. Unfortunately, this book's contributors are all-too familiar with poorly written and/or bland letters. To avoid this fate, you may want to suggest something specific for each of your recommenders to target. If each of their letters focuses on different aspects of your professional skills, you may more easily stand out from the crowd. For example, one might target your writing skills and ability to generate a strong, active research agenda. Another could address your field, highlighting a particular specialization. The third could comment on your interpersonal talents. In this way, your letters of recommendation and professional references should help the members of a search committee to see you as a highly competent professional, a person active in your field, with the potential to flourish in academia.

It's also worth noting that if you pass the first cut of the selection process, one or more of your recommenders will almost certainly be telephoned. It is therefore quite important that your recommenders be verbally competent and able to respond extemporaneously to questions about your suitability for a given position.

The following guide will help you to envision and organize your professional references and letters of recommendation. Note that you are not usually allowed to review your letters of recommendation. You can, however, have them sent to a file on campus and subsequently forwarded to an outside reviewer, who can verify that they are free of mistakes and troubling comments. Most career counseling centers will provide a file for your letters of recommendation and, upon request, forward them in support of your application packet. (See Table 9.)

TEACHING ARTIFACTS

Unless you are applying for a non-teaching academic position, you will want to include artifacts related to your effectiveness as a teacher. These may include syllabi, course outlines and lists of assignments, materials used in courses, technology, didactic means, non-traditional teaching approaches, etc. Also in this section should be others' attestations of your teaching effectiveness, such as letters written by faculty who have observed you, and data (both quantitative and qualitative) from student evaluations.

If you have taught multiple courses as a part of your doctoral work, or taught as an adjunct, or served at a university for several years, your packet may be lengthy. Care must be taken not to overwhelm (read: turn off) search-committee members. One strategy here is to introduce your mate-

	DR. JONES	DR. RENEE	DR. HELSEL	DR. SEDONA	DR. COUSER
Teaching	X				
Research	X				
Service		X			
Presentations					X
Collegiality				X	
Grant-writing		X			
Technology				X	
Diversity			X		
Community service			X		
Leadership	X				
Other:					

Table 9: Guide to recommendations

rials with a comprehensive, one or two page summary; you can then attach the above-listed items as supporting documents. (See Table 10.)

TEACHING PHILOSOPHY

In addition to providing evidence of its effectiveness, you will probably be asked to document the style and goals of your teaching—i.e., your philosophy. This statement should be clearly written and succinct, around one or two pages in length. You should describe your overall approach to teaching by presenting specific examples of methods by which you have reached students.

The following guide lists the parameters of most teaching-philosophy statements. In conjunction with this guide, we suggest a Google search to find examples of teaching philosophies in your specific discipline. You will find hundreds of good examples of wording, phrases, and construction. (See Table 11.)

TEACHING PORTFOLIO

Your teaching portfolio contains evidence that you can meet the expectations of a given position. Its first page is a cover sheet that directly links your evidence to the position's description:

	STUDENT EVALUATIONS (Overall effectivenss)	OBSERVATION LETTERS	STUDENT COMMENTS	TECHNOLOGY USED
Course A	5.8 (out of 6)	Please see letter from Dr. Ian Ryan	See appendix D	BlackBoard
Course B	5.4 (out of 6)		See appendix E	BlackBoard, PowerPoint, web cameras
Course C	5.7 (out of 6)	Please see letter from Dr. Meghan Will	See appendix F	BlackBoard
Course D	5.9 (out of 6)		See appendix G	BlackBoard
Course E	6.0 (out of 6)		See appendix H	BlackBoard

Table 10: Guide to teaching artifacts

QUESTION TO BE ANSWERED	WHAT YOU NEED TO INCLUDE	EXAMPLE
Why do you teach?	Your call to the teaching profession	"I teach because of the powerful impact I can have on future practitioners."
What are your objectives?	Internal and external goals	"One of my primary goals is to cultivate in my students the same love for the field and respect for diversity that my professors instilled in me."
How do you reach those objectives?	Techniques you use in your teaching	"Because different students learn in different ways, I infuse technology into each class session."
How do you measure performance?	Descriptions of the ways in which you gather and use data for improvement of your teaching	"Because many of our students sit for the national exam, I use the data compiled from this exam, in connection with feeback I receive from formal (end of semester) evaluations, to improve my teaching."
Other considerations	Items you might consider addressing in your statement	Technology, diversity, different learning styles, collaborations, ongoing training, making use of feedback

Table 11: Guide to teaching philosophy

Job Description: We seek a broadly trained sociologist; areas of specialization are open. The candidate should demonstrate excellence in teaching. As assistant professor, the successful candidate will teach both introductory and upper-division courses. Possible courses include Introduction to Sociology, Sociology of the Family, and Race and Ethnicity. The successful candidate may be asked to develop new courses or teach special topics that align with his or her areas of specialization.

As is evident, the teaching portfolio's cover sheet (see Figure 1) is directly anchored to the job description. This makes it easier for committee members to find data, understand your fit, and move your materials forward. Care must be taken not to overwhelm the committee with extensive documentation of your teaching performance.

During your on-campus visit, you will almost certainly be required to conduct a teaching demonstration; therefore, you may not want to describe your instructional prowess at length. You will have ample opportunity to demonstrate both your teaching skills and your underlying philosophy of pedagogy.

PROFESSIONAL WRITING

Professional writing—i.e., authoring articles for peer-reviewed journals and the like—can enlarge your professional network and, even beyond the

ITEM	DESCRIPTION	EVIDENCE
Excellence in teaching	I have been targeting a teaching career for many years. My primary goal in my studies has been to learn new and effective ways to reach students.	• Teaching evaluations • Observations by faculty • Sample syllabus and associated assignment sheets
Introductory courses	I have taught each of the core introductory classes at the University of America.	• "Course Taught" section of vitae
Upper-level courses	I have taught or co-taught several upper-level courses at the University of America.	• "Course Taught" section of vitae • Letter of recommendation from Dr. Burns
"Introduction to Sociology"	I taught this course during the Fall 2011 semester.	• Student evaluations • Syllabus
"Sociology of the Family"	I taught this course during the Spring 2012 semester.	• Student evaluations • Observation letter from Dr. Smith • Syllabus
Race and ethnicity	I cover race and ethnicity in each of my courses.	• Syllabi • Course assignments
Development of new courses	I co-developed a new course, "Sociology in the 21st Century," for the Spring 2006 semester. This course is now part of the core curriculum.	• Syllabus • Letter of recommenation from Dr. Jones

Figure 1: Teaching portfolio cover sheet

recognition you receive from your peers, will be a definite positive to the search committee. A committee member might have very different opinions regarding the suitability of someone who gives evidence of an active research agenda and another who suggests only the potential for same. Remember, many regional and state journals are constantly seeking articles for publication; such venues offer clear opportunities for your research and writing. Your doctoral dissertation may provide exactly what you need to break into print, and by collaborating with faculty members who've published before, you will greatly increase the possibility of your manuscript being accepted. Aside from peer-reviewed journals, professional magazines and newsletters also offer opportunities for you to publish professionally.

If you have not been published when you begin composing your packet, you can still document your progress on substantial writing projects: perhaps you're turning your dissertation into an article, or working on a paper that was written for class but has publication potential. If you are developing a manuscript, indicate in your materials that the work is in progress; you will, of course, need to be prepared to talk about your plans for publication during the campus interview. Identifying a journal and setting a timeline for completion of the manuscript may be helpful, here.

RESEARCH AGENDA AND METHODOLOGY

Members of the search committee are naturally quite interested in projecting the role you would play as part of their department. Accordingly, they may ask you for a written statement of your research interests, current research projects, long-range plans for researching an area or subject, and your preferred approach to researching a question. They may also want to discover your general areas of methodological expertise (e.g., quantitative or qualitative). As with your statement of teaching philosophy, this document should be clearly written and concise—we suggest no more than one page.

> SAMPLE: My research agenda is anchored to the further understanding of racial and ethnic diversity. Racial and ethnic diversity includes Whites, Blacks, Hispanics, Asians, American Indians, Middle Eastern Americans, and multi-racial individuals. My research interests focus on understanding in greater depth the merging of behavioral, affective, and institutional implications of diversity. My primary goal is to promote increased knowledge

about how variation in racial and ethnic diversity manifests in career decision-making. My research agenda enlarges the existing research by broadening the focus to include multiple racial and ethnic groups. Additionally, my agenda attempts to suggest best practices in career development means and measures for minority culture members. Because of the nature of my questions, my agenda utilizes both quantitative and qualitative research methods.

SERVICE-ORIENTED ACTIVITIES

This category is quite broad by nature. Generally, service-oriented activities are those that employ your specialized knowledge for the betterment of the community (and beyond); this can include contributions to certain committees on the campus, in the community, and at the state or national level. It's important to take stock of your history in this area, because the search committee is not only looking for a competent academic performer, but for a good citizen as well. Furthermore, the committee will need to know that you can willingly perform this type of work if it is part of the university's promotion and tenure requirements.

PROFESSIONAL PRESENTATIONS

One of the best ways to introduce yourself to your field at large is through presentations at state, regional, or national conferences. Whether you present a paper via a poster presentation or in a session, your peers will be in attendance. Such exposure can be extremely valuable for professional growth and networking.

Other forms of professional presentations—usually less costly in time, money, or both—involve meeting with campus or community organizations that can benefit from your expertise.

You should note professional presentations in your vitae and cover letter, and be sure to keep copies of handouts (and other pertinent material) to document your efforts.

COVER LETTER

Search-committee members are quite likely to be charged with the task of combing through dozens and dozens of letters. This book's authors know from experience that when faced with a mountain of application materials, search-committee members start by weeding out as many applicants as possible. Whatever fails to make a strong first impression is quickly excised. Let us emphasize that these committee members are not meeting and evaluating you in the flesh: they are meeting you via your paper credentials, and if the materials you forward to them are not aligned as closely as possible with the position announcement, then—no matter how wonderful and deserving you are—you are unlikely to advance to the next step.

The process usually goes something like this: First, the university's Human Resources department or the departmental secretary ascertains that each candidate's application materials are complete. Completed packets are forwarded to the chair of the search committee (or some other repository), where they may lie dormant for an indeterminate period of time. After the deadline for completed packets has passed, those that are eligible are distributed to the committee for individual evaluation. Using a previously arranged system, each committee member rates all the candidates (that is, all the packets). (See Table 12.)

It is crucial that your application materials get a good initial rating. How good a rating do you need? If the university is planning to interview three candidates, you need to be in the top three. If the university is going all the way to five, then you must be one of the top five. Hence, one of the most important documents you will submit during this entire process is your cover letter. Your cover letter must captivate your audience, get them interested in learning more about you, and make them begin to see that you are the person for whom this position was created.

Your letter should, of course, provide your contact information: name, address, phone number, and email. It should also identify the exact advertisement to which you're responding. Name the job and, if listed in the posting, its number.

Your letter must highlight your qualifications regarding each of the position's specific requirements. Omitting significant expectations here is an invitation to search-committee members to quickly screen you out. Take great pains to compose your letter in a way that is both clear and interesting to the reader.

Since you will probably apply for more than one position, you may want to start by drafting a general cover letter. You can adjust the contents of this base model to fit the particulars of each posting to which you respond.

	WHAT THE SEARCHER IS DOING	WHAT THE SEARCH COMMITTEE IS DOING
September	• Developing skeletal application materials (cover letter, vitae, etc.) • Searching online and print materials for job postings • Contacting references and network for possible openings	• Creating and finalizing job posting • Developing review instruments (initial paper review, phone interview, and campus visit
October	• Searching for positions • Tuning application materials	• Forwarding job advertisement and review instruments to Human Resources and /or Social Equity for approval
November	• Fitting skeletal materials to posted job advertisements • Sending completed applications to job openings	• Posting job advertisement • Reviewing application materials
December	• Continuing to send completed applications to job openings • Following up on materials to make sure packets are complete	• Individually rating, then discussing as a group, the list of completed applications • Creating an initial short-list of applicants (3-6) to invite for phone interviews
January	• Continuing to check for and apply to additional openings • Interviewing via phone	• Scheduling and conducting phone interviews with short-list
February	• Attending campus interviews • Continuing to check for and apply to openings	• Scheduling and conduction on-campus interviews (typically 2-3 candidates) • Submitting a rank-ordered list of candidates for hire to administration (including documentation of why applicants were not considered)
March	• Negotiating and accepting position • Or, continuing to apply and interview	• Receiving final approval from administration (administration, usually the dean, negotiates with applicant)

Table 12: Guide to search timeline

We strongly suggest that your letter mirror the posting. For example, if the posting lists research duties first, then your training, strengths, and experience in research should be the first topic you cover. If teaching requirements come second, put them second.

NOTE:

Search committees are made up of human beings. Anything in your paper presentation that helps them see through the clutter they face as they sift through literally thousands of pages of material—in short, anything you do that makes their job easier—is almost always to your benefit. Allow your qualifications to shine through as clearly and distinctly as possible. Allow them to sparkle.

VITAE

Another critical factor in your candidacy is, of course, your vitae. Your vitae must communicate your eminent and unquestionable qualifications. Hopefully, each committee member will review it carefully.

Often, the more closely your vitae mirrors the job posting, the higher your score during the initial culling. Matching your vitae to expectations is important because while your vitae will not get you the job, it must be solid enough to get you to the next stage. If you are a college basketball fan, think of March Madness (the NCAA tournament): When your paper credentials arrive on campus, you are one of sixty-four aspirants. You can break out of the crowd by aligning your materials as closely as possible to the expectations of the position. By scoring highly on whatever rubric the committee uses, you can make the Final Four. Keep in mind that the function of your vitae is not to get you the job, but to advance you to the interview stage.

Some searchers mail fifty to a hundred vitae. If this is your strategy, great care must still be taken to tailor each version of your vitae to the position for which you're applying. For example, you may read a job posting for someone with experience in area X. Perhaps you have limited experience directly related to X and, consequently, you refer to it only briefly, near the end of your vitae. Returning to our basketball analogy, unless you move the X area up and legitimately bolster it, you're giving yourself a seed of sixty or so in the sixty-four-team field. You will easily be excluded from further consideration, which is the worst way for you to lighten the committee's load. To make matters worse, you'll have wasted some paper, some ink, some postage, and probably some emotion over the enterprise.

Remember that when you're submitting your vitae, so are thirty, forty, or seventy other PhD holders; your goal is no less than to convince every member of the selection committee (at least, those paying attention) that you should be one of the few candidates advancing to the second round. Half-measures will eat up time and won't succeed.

NOTE:

Unfortunately, not all committee members are particularly assiduous. One of this book's authors served on a committee in which a co-member did not do his homework. When the committee began to discuss the candidates in earnest, this member blurted out, "Oh my goodness, that person is my boss!" Obviously, the member in question had not

Figure 2 is a skeletal vitae outline.

Before sending your materials, carefully review the advertisement to make sure you've included everything it requests. The completion and submission of all required materials prior to the deadline is totally your responsibility. Sadly, each of this book's authors has served on search committees that were unable to consider known candidates because they lacked some document or missed the deadline.

FOLLOWING UP

Some schools will let you know whether they've received all of your materials; in other cases, you'll need to follow up to make sure your packet arrived intact and the school needs nothing else from you. Following up isn't required, and you should know that schools can take a long time to respond to applicants' materials—sometimes months. Nevertheless, since the responsibility for sending a complete packet is yours, not your prospective employers, it's possible for you to be excluded from the applicant pool because your cover letter never made it into your file, or because one of the required references was not received. That's another way in which you'd rather not lighten the search committee's load.

Moreover, following up on your application might make the committee see you as genuinely enthusiastic about the position. If committee members know you're interested in them, they'll probably be a bit more interested in seeing what you have to offer. In this vein, following up gives you the opportunity to make a human connection with a committee mem-

PERSONAL INFORMATION

Name, address, phone, email
(Optional information: date of birth, place of birth, citizenship, gender,
marital status, number of children)

EDUCATION

List your degrees in chronological order from latest to earliest. You may include additional training specific to the position or to your field.

Example: PhD, Teacher Education, University of America

DISSERTATION TITLE

The title of your dissertation and date or expected date of defense. You may also list the names of your committee members.

Example: The Examination of a Performance-based Assessment of 7th Grade Science Teachers

EMPLOYMENT HISTORY

Listed in chronological order, from latest to earliest. Include: time for which you held the position, your title, the university or organization, and several key words or phrases that capture the essence of what you did.

Example: 2003—2005: Graduate Teaching Assistant, the University of America; taught courses, evaluated papers, created and scored tests

2000—2003: CEO, Fish Industrial Solutions; managed personnel, handled budget, established business contacts

COURSES TAUGHT

Indicate dates, name(s), and institution(s).

Example: Spring, 2004: GEO 310: Introduction to Hydrogeology
Fall 2005: GEO 400: Geomorphology

RESEARCH

Date(s), name(s) of project(s), methodology.

Example: 2003-2006: The Investigation of Invertebrates in French Creek, Quantitative

A Phenomenological Study of College Students' Drinking Patterns

CONSULTING

Date(s), topic(s), place(s).

Example: Fall, 2005: Role of educational leaders in developing a K-12 curriculum (American High School)

PROFESSIONAL QUALIFICATIONS

Specific certifications or credentials related to your field and the position. You may also list specific licenses.

Example: Certified Public Accountant

Licensed Social Worker

AWARDS

Those related to your field or the position. You may include scholarships or fellowships.

Example: 2004: Outstanding Graduate Student Award; College of America

Figure 2: Vitae outline

PUBLICATIONS

All publications (refereed and non-refereed) in chronological order from latest to earliest. You may also note works in progress.

Example:

Smith, J. A. Infusing information technologies into the classroom: A Mixed-method study of the impact of IT in land-grant Institutions. *The Journal of Information Technology* 23 (2005): 4.

Jones, P. How nursing has evolved through the years: A content analysis of the journal of nursing (1971-2005). *The Journal of Nursing.* (In press)

Doe, J. A *Study of the Impact of Foreign Workers on State Economies.* (In process)

PRESENTATIONS

All the presentations in which you've participated. Separating this section may make sense if you've given refereed (e.g., professional conference) and non-refereed (e.g., asked to speak at a local high school) presentations. Make note of those events to which you were invited. Include date, topic, place, name(s) of co-presenter(s).

Example: "Collaborations across disciplines: Why business leaders should consider unique connections." Iowa Business Conference (Des Moines, Iowa: April 23, 2006). Co-presented with Katie Wilson.

GRANTS

All of the grants you have applied for and/or received. Include: year, name of project, name of funding source, amount requested, amount received.

Example: 2007. Bringing Music to Inner-city Youth, the Jefferson County Chamber of Commerce. Requested: $2,500. Received: $2,500.

SERVICE

All of your committee and volunteer work. You may separate this category into university and community subcategories.

Example: 2004—2006: University of America, Member, Social Equity Advisory Group

2004—2007: United Way of Green Bay, Volunteer

PROFESSIONAL MEMBERSHIPS

Professional organizations of which your are, or have been, a member. Spell out acronyms.

Example: 2004—Current: APA (American Psychological Association)

2002—2007: RMPA (Rocky Mountain Psychological Association)

INTERESTS

There is value in letting people know things about you (within reason) that they may find a connection with.

Example: Hiking, painting, running, poetry

REFERENCES

Names of references; alternately, indicate that references are available upon request. If listing references, be sure to include name, phone, email, address, institution/organization.

Figure 2: Vitae outline, con't

ber, which can mean a lot. Taking the time—and summoning the courage —to call the committee chair pays off with a chance to break the ice, and maybe have a conversation about your qualifications.

THE POSTING

Most universities conduct national searches for academic positions, which entails placing ads that will reach the largest possible number of applicants. As mentioned above, internet sources like HigherEdJobs.com and chroniclecareers.com are good places to look. You'll also want to check journals and publications in your field, and look to your friends, colleagues, family, and professors. (See Figure 3.)

You can usually gather a lot of information from a position announcement. Pay close attention to the order in which job requirements are listed, and to how the position's duties are described. In our example, the search committee is clearly looking for candidates who value teaching above all else. Although they want someone who can produce professional writing and presentations, as well as perform service activities, the primary focus is pedagogy: it's emphasized in the sections on job duties, qualifications, and application materials. Furthermore, you can tell that if you were hired by this institution you'd be working in a fairly large department and have many colleagues in your area (you could confirm this by checking the website or making a phone call).

Note the value placed on being a good fit—the committee is looking for someone whose interests are similar to those of the other faculty. This is common and not insignificant. With a quick online search, it should be easy to discover which, if any, faculty members share your research/service affinities. That knowledge may prove quite valuable during the many exchanges of the search process. Obviously, the more positive and fruitful your communications with members of the search committee, the greater your chance of being offered the position.

After reading five or ten job advertisements, you'll start to notice subtle differences in wording that lend more weight to some requirements than others. It's very important for you take the time and effort to decipher the clues that indicate what search committees are really saying.

Following (Figure 4) is an example of how a committee might plot its requirements onto a rating sheet. Using a rating sheet allows the committee to reduce a mountain of application materials to manageable dimensions. After each member has read and rated the applications, the

INSTITUTION: University A
LOCATION: Anytown, USA
POSTED: 10/20/11
APPLICATION DUE: 1/24/12
START DATE: 8/25/12

JOB DUTIES: Teach undergraduate and graduate courses (4 per semester) in [_____] with a primary emphasis on [_____] and specialized courses in [_____]. We will favorably consider applicants with teaching experience in [_____] area. In addition to teaching responsibilities, applicants will be expected to conduct and publish high-quality research and participate in both university and community service activities.

QUALIFICATIONS: Demonstrated excellence in teaching and the ability to work both cooperatively and productively with colleagues and students. An established or potential research agenda in [_____]. A doctoral degree in [_____] must be completed by the start date. Favorable applicants will have a history of research in areas similar to existing faculty, as well as work experience in [_____].

DEPARTMENT: The department is the largest in the College of [_____]. The faculty are dedicated to the art of teaching, engage in collegial collaboration on academic projects, and take pride in student-centered relationships.

UNIVERSITY: University A was founded in 1927 as a land-grant institution. It is a Carnegie Doctoral/Research-Extensive university. It has an enrollment of 22,000 students, representing all 50 states and, on average, 42 nationalities. The university offers 90 master's degrees and 23 doctoral degrees. University A is accredited by NCATE; the department is accredited by [_____].

APPLICATION: Applicants are asked to submit the following materials: cover letter addressing teaching philosophy, with a detailed vitae highlighting scholarly accomplishments; evidence of excellence in teaching; research interests/ background; and names and contact numbers of at least five references.

Figure 3: Sample job posting

committee will meet as a group to determine which candidates appear most viable. Some of the numerical ratings may be adjusted based on certain members' salient observations. Finally—through what is, admittedly, an imperfect method—a narrow applicant pool is chosen.

NETWORKING

The people you know in your field can offer significant assistance in your job search. Since academic circles are often small, the earlier you begin developing your personal network, the better. Your primary network is made

---

EVALUATION FORM

Name of Applicant: _____ Date evaluated: _____

Evaluated by: _____

Required qualifications (check if identified):

_____ **Doctorate (Discipline-specific)**

Review Transcript

_____ **Active Research Agenda**

Publications in peer-reviewed journals

Publications in press

Publications in progress

Preferred qualifications (use scale of 1-7, 1 being low and 7 being high)

_____ **Teaching Experience**

1 year or less = 1

1-2 years = 2

3-5 years = 3

6-9 years = 5

10-15 years = 6

over 15 years = 7

_____ **Teaching Quality**

Teaching awards

Details contained in recommendation letters from students and colleagues

Student course-evaluation data

_____ **Serving Students**

Openness and positive demeanor with students

Expressed interest in students' academic and overall well-being

Consistency and accountability in interacting with students included in recommendation letters and telephone conversations

_____ **Ensuring Student Learning**

Perceived ability to identify and remove obstacles from student learning

Expressed interest in seeing students succeed

_____ **Maintaining High Standards for Students, Program, and Self**

Sample syllabi

Other instructional materials

Information gained through reference letters

_____ **Course, Curriculum, Program Development**

Vitae

Sample syllabi

Other instructional materials

Information gained through reference letters

Figure 4: Sample review form

_____ **Scholarly Accomplishments**
Publications
Manuscripts in press
Manuscripts in progress
Presentations at professional meetings
_____ **Professional Service**
Vitae
Letters of recommendation
_____ **Knowledge in Discipline**
Information gained from vitae
Letters (candidate's and others)
_____ **Experience in Discipline**
Information gained from vitae
Letters (candidate's and others)
Comments: _____

Figure 4: Sample review form, con't

up of faculty in your department (whether you are their colleague or student); cultivating positive relationships with them helps dramatically when you start your search, as one of their names on a letter of recommendation or list of references can go a long way toward getting you a campus interview.

Beyond this immediate circle is the larger network of your discipline. To gain access to this network, you can attend state, regional, and national conferences, each of which promotes networking through scheduled activities, job- and vitae-posting services, and informal chances to mingle. You can also attend professional conferences as a presenter: many organizations accept nearly 100 percent of poster-presentation submissions, though paper presentations are usually more competitive. State conferences often accept student papers and research.

Whether you are simply attending a conference or presenting research, you should take the opportunity to connect with as many professionals in your field as possible. It is difficult sometimes to attend the "meet and greet" hour of the conference, but that hour can really pay off: it enables the professionals you encounter to put your face and words with your soon-to-be-arriving application materials. On your end, you'll have the chance to meet potential colleagues and, through their personalities and presentations, informally size up their programs. In some instances, the information you pick up during even these relatively brief encounters will reinforce your initially positive thoughts about a program; in other instances, it will confirm that the program wouldn't be a good fit. Thus, you will narrow your search and broaden your potential for success.

CHAPTER 4

The Interview Process

Academic professionals often attribute their being hired to their performance during the interview. It is true that the interview is immensely important; in fact, it is probably the most important single factor of the entire employment process. However, rarely is it the *sole* determinant of a candidate's fate. The candidate is usually provided many other opportunities to prove his or her mettle.

THE PRE-PROCESS (PHONE INTERVIEW)

As noted earlier, candidates under serious consideration for a campus visit will be asked to take part in a phone interview. These interviews serve multiple purposes for both the committee and the candidate. The university wants to invite only candidates who are definitely interested in the position, and a telephone interchange can help them determine the candidate's true interest level—as well as, in some cases, the candidate's suitability. Of course, if the search committee has been really conscientious in its work, most, if not all, of the candidates called will be invited to the campus for further screening. But that is not a forgone conclusion. Sometimes the committee will eliminate a candidate based on a questionable phone performance, and sometimes the tenor of the interview will prompt a candidate to withdraw his or her name.

For example, one of this book's authors had a phone interview that seemed to go oddly from the very beginning. He enjoys using humor to make personal connections, and sensed that this trait wasn't buzzing over the phone lines. Twenty minutes into the interview, it suddenly became evident that the committee was looking for a somewhat serious, definitely research-oriented, conservative individual. The author didn't fit that bill, so with both respect and decisiveness, he thanked the committee members and ended the interview.

Although it may appear at first blush that something went wrong here, such occurrences are actually win-win. The committee won by not having to expend further time and money on a candidate whose strengths and interests lay in areas other than those the university wanted. The candidate won by recognizing that this particular position was not a good personal or professional fit.

During your phone interview, you may find that not everyone on the committee is on the other end of the line; nevertheless, the interview will follow a standard protocol. You will be asked to respond to the same questions posed to every other candidate still in the running. Your answers will likely be scored by each member of the committee for later comparison. Naturally, your score will be determined primarily by how you address the true intent of each question. It is also likely to be affected by the subjective interests and bent of each committee member. For this reason, it's important to listen carefully—not only to grasp the content of the questions, but to attempt to pick up clues as to the interests or biases of the questioners. Then, should the opportunity arise, you can strengthen your candidacy by introducing or reinforcing anything you have in common with the committee. We do advise caution, here, as pandering will be easily read as a negative.

At the end, the committee will give you the chance to ask some questions of your own. While the university is seeking an employee, this is also your job search. It goes without saying that what you ask the committee members should reflect your interest in the position, department, faculty, university, etc. Your questions should be drawn from the list you compiled prior to being called by the committee.

THE CAMPUS (INTERVIEW) PROCESS

One of the most important steps in attaining your job is a successful campus visit. During this time, candidates typically face exten-

NOTE:

Sometimes, of course, a committee will decide to contact a candidate only to find that he or she has already accepted a position elsewhere. This is a real problem when committees take excessively long periods of time to evaluate credentials and make their preliminary decisions on the pool of candidates. They often lose very promising people because of such delays.

sive meetings, which can be somewhat grueling. Depending on the university or department, the experience may range from one to three days. Most campus interviews follow a schedule similar to the one described below.

MONDAY

3:45 p.m. – arrive at airport (met by two committee members)

5:15 p.m. – arrive at hotel

6:00 p.m. – dinner with members of search committee

TUESDAY

8:00 a.m. – breakfast with committee members

9:00 a.m. – meet with dean

9:45 a.m. – meet with assistant provost

10:30 a.m. – break

11:00 a.m. – research presentation to students and search committee

12:00 p.m. – lunch with committee members

1:00 p.m. – meet with department chair

2:00 p.m. – interview with search committee

3:00 p.m. – break

3:30 p.m. – teaching presentation

4:30 p.m. – meeting with Human Resources

As you can see, these visits are packed with meetings and usually interspersed with breakfasts, lunches, and possibly a dinner or two. The time frame is tight because not only is the university allocating financial resources to your visit, but staff members are being called to devote considerable periods of time and effort over and above their usual duties. Remember that you are only one of several candidates; both the university and the department want the best look they can get for their time and money.

In recognition of the great gravity and expenditure surrounding the hiring event, it's essential that you appreciate, from the moment you arrive to the moment you finally depart, that you will have many, many opportunities to advance your candidacy and impress the people you may one day work with: various search committee members, a dean or two, the vice-provost, the department secretary, students, and anyone else you run into on campus or in the community. Even if you feel you should be judged on nothing but your professional acumen, it probably won't be all that simple. You'll be evaluated almost every step of the way.

MEALS

The meals you share with committee members offer all of you the chance to experience each other in a social situation, which helps answer questions like: How do you fit in? How do they appear to you? Do you appear to be someone with whom they can work? Have you identified certain faculty members who seem to share some of your real research interests?

You may have few meals during your entire life as important as those you share with these people, and you must be prepared to juggle several concerns. You'll need to engage in meal-friendly conversation on topics ranging from local activities to sports to your flight and, almost certainly, to department and university issues. The tone may range from informal to serious—that is, interview-like. Let the committee members lead the way. Whatever the tone, try to be yourself. Be genuine.

Since, as noted above, members of search committees often invest a lot of time and effort on top of their normal schedules, enjoying a good meal at one of the better restaurants in town may, for them, represent a pleasant reward. Furthermore, it gives them an opportunity to socialize with others from the department. If the event allows you to pose some questions in a relaxed manner, it probably won't hurt your chances, and may enhance them.

Conversely, one of the authors, while serving as a member of a search committee, witnessed a candidate who, though he interviewed well and possessed skills and qualifications that were easily as strong as the other candidates', decided for some reason that dinner was the time to demonstrate his adeptness at monopolizing the table conversation. This proved detrimental to his cause, as one of the search-committee members (not our author) also happened to enjoy controlling dinner discourse. The ensuing sparring match took place right in front of the rest of the committee. It was later discussed during the final evaluation of the candidate. He was not offered the position, perhaps in part because of what transpired during the meal.

Without a doubt, sharing meals with committee members—as well as trips to and from the airport, campus tours, shuttles between offices, and the like—are opportunities to ask important questions about the position, the department, the university, and the local area. Information you pick up can go a long way toward helping you decide whether or not this is the position for you. You might also begin to understand department initiatives, issues, and things of interest that you'll be able to weave into later conversations and your answers to questions. Such tidbits of information will demonstrate to the dean, provost, assistant provost, department chair, and search committee that you've been paying close attention and are completely engaged.

Notwithstanding the importance of these ancillary factors, your fate will be determined primarily by your performances during the series of scheduled meetings and presentations packed into your campus visit, each of which is discussed below in the order of its appearance on our hypothetical schedule.

MEETING WITH THE DEAN

The dean is usually somewhat different from the other faculty members you bump into on your campus sojourn. For one thing, he or she is one step removed from the classroom and, although interested in your ability to carry out that particular part of your job, really has other things at the top of the agenda. Keep in mind that in the normal course of events, a competent dean has a full plate of responsibilities, some of which involve personnel management—think "problem professors." Consequently, the dean's main goal in meeting with you is probably to place you somewhere on a continuum whose poles are labeled "Asset to the University" and "Problem for the University (or me—the Dean)." Stated in the simplest terms, if you appear "weak," "some sort of loose cannon," or "a poor fit," (and the dean is the *only* person who can define these terms), you represent a potential problem. When discussing your candidacy, particularly with the president, the dean may argue that your name be red-lined.

That said, your meeting with the dean is not likely to destroy your candidacy, unless you exhibit some really foolish or tactless behaviors (e.g., announcing that, in your considered opinion, administrators are generally lacking in intelligence and overpaid). Nor are you likely to get the position based solely on the fact that you impressed the dean with your repartee. Just avoid saying anything that might hurt your viability as a candidate. You may already have picked up some hints about the dean's biases by paying careful attention during earlier interactions with the people you met on campus, or even from people you know who also know the dean.

Recognize that deans are usually skilled at conducting meetings and highly interested in taking the lead. Following his or her prompts may be your best bet. Of course, should the dean broach an area of interest that you share, whether it be a certain management style or the Pittsburgh Steelers, you should voice your views.

Finally, it will not hurt your chances here (or anywhere else during this process) if the dean decides that you are not only competent, but a likable person.

> Example: One of this book's authors once posed the following question to a person he considered the finest administrator he had ever worked with: "Assume two candidates are equal in virtually every way, but you have to choose only one. How would you do it?"
>
> "I'd pick the one I liked better," he answered, without a moment's hesitation.

MEETINGS WITH THE ASSISTANT PROVOST, PROVOST, VICE-PRESIDENT, ETC.

All the observations that pertain to the dean hold true here. One important wrinkle, however, is that while search-committee members need to be impressed by your capability and suitability for the position, in the end the only thing they can do is either recommend that you be considered or decide not to forward your name. The usual process involves the committee forwarding your name along with several others. More often than not, they will submit those names in rank order, hopefully with yours on top, to the president of the university. Then the president, probably following consultation with key campus officials—the dean, vice provost, etc.—makes the final selection.

Therefore, meeting with any of these key administrative officials can (and probably will) result in either a positive or negative tilt to your chances. You can bet that their counsel will not be taken lightly. Do your best to present yourself *honestly* and *professionally*. Above all, do not burn any bridges.

RESEARCH PRESENTATION

Whether the position you've applied for is research oriented, teaching oriented, or a combination of both, you will probably be required to present your research findings to an assembled group. This is a "two- or three-for" for the university, because your audience is likely to consist of both students and faculty members. The faculty may be some of those who are free from other duties at the scheduled time. The students will probably fall into two categories: those who have been asked there by interested faculty members, who will later solicit the students' input regarding your potential, and other students who happen to be free and curious. You might also find a stray administrator, secretary, or other staff member, but that is less likely.

This experience affords you the opportunity to demonstrate your research expertise to a professional group. There are a number of ways to approach it. You can attempt to play the role of the all-knowing expert—that is, to blow your audience away with reams of handouts and a quarter-mile of overheads or PowerPoint slides. Your authors have encountered this kind of presentation, which sometimes ends up demonstrating more about ego than research. You could also decide to address only those parts of your material that can be easily reduced to a PowerPoint presentation, in which case you'll pass around some handouts and hope that no one has any really penetrating or controversial responses. In this instance, the phrase "went over like a lead balloon," or something similar, may later appear on the critique sheets.

You're probably better off targeting your presentation somewhere between these extremes, in a comfortable place that allows you to demonstrate your expertise while allowing your audience to help drive the discussion. It's unlikely that any members of your audience will know more about your specific area of research than you do. It is likely, however, that members of the group will have something to say about it. Some, in fact, may have conducted research on the same topic, and you should make sure that their knowledge shows through. Otherwise, you risk alienating people who will later voice their opinions as to whether you should be hired. Along those lines, if your research is anchored in Theory A and several members of your audience are conducting similar research using Theory B, and you go out of your way to discount Theory B, then you've gone a long way toward securing the position for some other candidate.

Should your audience appear to have little real knowledge of your topic, care must be taken not to come off as if, having arrived at the university, you'll shine so brightly that your colleagues will look inept. This is more likely to be a concern in fields that are currently advancing quickly. For example, some of the "old guard" who have trouble sending and receiving email may not be particularly thrilled by someone glibly extolling his or her ease with writing computer programs. While that example may be a bit extreme, the point remains: do not turn your research presentation into a negative by coming across as being beyond the scope of the faculty. Remember that this process is designed, in part, to determine how well you would fit in and advance the professional efforts of the department as a whole; you don't want to outrun everyone in the room. If you are selected, you will have plenty of time to prove your worth.

Of course, it's also a mistake to approach this presentation with the fear that you are some sort of imposter, just because your research project (dissertation) is not absolutely perfect. Most hiring committees are made up either solely or predominately of faculty members, many of whom will still be able to recall how they felt when they went through the search process. They will not expect you to know everything about any subject; they're human beings, and know that they're not built that way either. Most of these people are simply looking for a competent colleague, especially one who gives evidence that he or she can be effectively and professionally mentored. Allow them to see that you are genuinely interested in being a mentee.

When presenting research, it is crucial to understand and relate to your audience. While you may have faculty members with sophisticated knowledge in the general area of your presentation, who will want to hear you discuss advanced theory in the subject, you will also have students whose understanding is more limited. Honor the students' level and interest, and attempt to present the material in a way that both includes and enlightens them. Your employment probably depends more on how well you communicate with students than how effectively you relate to a specific faculty member, no matter how challenging and exciting the exchange might be for the two of you.

Finally, you should be prepared to field some very tough questions that may or may not support your research. Here it is important that your responses be both accurate and diplomatic.

TEACHING PRESENTATION

If the research presentation lets you exercise some of your classroom skills, the teaching presentation is the time for those skills to really shine. This often-abridged version of a class session will be attended by faculty and students from the department, and maybe some faculty from allied departments. Your goal should be to reach and teach all of them.

The search committee will later be extremely interested in the students' opinions of your teaching abilities, since, as noted above, they've probably asked some of the department's best and brightest to attend the session. Not only is the committee interested in hiring a competent and professional colleague, it also wants a person who knows how to interact with students.

MEETING WITH THE DEPARTMENT CHAIR

Department chairs come in many varieties. Some have been in the position for years, while others are new. Some are highly respected; some, less highly. There are those who exude energy and those who appear low-key. And there are many, many more who function somewhere between these extremes.

How can you know? Valuable insight can be gleaned from quizzing some of your knowledgeable off-campus acquaintances. Maybe your academic advisor or one of your recommenders has met the chair and has some feelings regarding him or her (remember, most professional circles are subsets of subsets of subsets.) As noted earlier, various people you've already met on campus may have provided you with some cues or shared some opinions about the chair. Regardless of what information you receive, file it under nice-to-know, not need-to-know; in meeting with the chair, what's most important is that you convey a sense of who and what you are, professionally and personally. You need to demonstrate your high degree of competence and indicate that you are an effective educator, a competent professional, a team player, and a self-starter. By this point in the process, you should have already exhibited a certain level of collegiality, both in meetings and less formal settings.

At the same time, it is important for you to convey that you will welcome professional mentoring. Your personal philosophy of ongoing, constant learning should be evident to the chair.

INTERVIEW WITH THE SEARCH COMMITTEE

Finally (at least on our schedule) comes a critical event: your audience with the actual departmental search committee. This event may well arrive at just the time you would like to return to your hotel, kick off your shoes, and turn on some escapist television. Instead, the schedule gets turned up a notch. You can think of this as a simple series of questions posed by a group of faculty members. The core questions were developed by the departmental committee and various offices on campus (including Human Resources and, possibly, Social Equity), and will be asked to every candidate in the same order, by the same committee member. Occasionally, committee members will ask extemporaneous questions in order to get further clarification on a candidate's answer.

Both your communication skills and your aplomb under pressure will be tested here. Of course, you will have practiced (out loud and with a friend or colleague who will give you honest critique) answering anticipated questions.

Many have found the following technique invaluable: Listen carefully to the question, making absolutely sure you understand what is being asked. Then pause and take a moment to consider what the questioner (committee) really wants to know. Then frame your answer and respond. If a follow-up is asked, try not to become defensive. Simply repeat the above process.

Example: In a job interview, one of the authors was asked a follow-up question about his predominant theory base. Although the questioner did not really appear to understand the theory, the follow-up query *was* an attempt to connect. Had the author decided in the moment that an attempt was being made to slip him up, he might have become defensive. After briefly pondering his response, how-

NOTE:

Even if you get a sense that a question is being added or further amplification is being requested, do not automatically conclude that you are doing poorly and panic. The committee member may simply be interested in having you provide more information about a topic because he or she has really reacted positively to your first response.

ever, the author answered by thanking the questioner for his interest and knowledge of the theory, and embedded in his response a modification of the question which honored the intent of the questioner and actually led to what the author judged as further productive discussion.

During this part of the process, members of the committee will be trying to get a real feel for who you are. Although you will have already had various interactions with individual department members, this may be the only instance of the entire committee sharing a formal, organized time with you. When the committee convenes one, two, three, or four weeks later to evaluate all the candidates, they may anchor the majority of their comments by reference to answers, behaviors, tone, intuitions, and the like that surfaced during this shared experience. Common reactions among the committee members will probably carry more weight than any brilliant observations you shared with a single committee member as he or she drove you to the airport. So, over and above all the facts that may have surfaced during the process, the interview provides the opportunity for you to show committee members what you are all about.

Now, your ego would prefer that you were offered every job you applied for, but your true goal should be to place yourself in the best possible position, professionally. You are more likely to succeed in this goal if you give clear evidence of who you really are, rather than who you think the committee wants you to be. Genuine responses are more memorable than contrived, canned responses.

It is customary at the end of the interview for the committee to ask whether you have any questions.

Of course you do.

And although you may have some based on the interview itself, below is a list of questions the authors have posed (you may also have asked some of these questions during interactions other than the committee interview):

NOTE:

It might help you navigate this process to take a moment and think of the pressure faced by the committee. Above all, they do not want to make a mistake. They are seeking a person who will be an asset to the university, one they can work with, who is a team player, a person committed to professional growth, and who can be mentored. The last thing the committee wants is to have to repeat the search process next year because their choice, for whatever reason, worked out poorly.

1. How are decisions made within the department?

2. What are the departmental guidelines regarding promotion and tenure, especially as they relate to teaching, publishing, presenting, and service?

3. How would you describe the typical student in your program?

4. What courses are you expecting the person selected for this position to teach?

5. What resources are available from the department/university for professional enhancement in teaching, research, and service?

6. How did this position become available?

7. What is the strategic plan for the university over the next five or ten years?

8. What is the economic health of the surrounding communities?

9. What colleges/universities in the area are competition?

10. How are new faculty mentored in the department?

POSSIBLE INTERVIEW QUESTIONS

Although we can't begin to identify all the questions you might be asked during an interview, those that follow should give you some feel for what to expect:

- What would you like to teach?
- How have you handled difficult students?
- How does your research inform your teaching?
- What are your research plans?
- Why did you apply here?
- What really gets you excited in the field?
- What will you bring to the department?
- What do you do outside of work?
- Where do you see yourself professionally in five years?
- What is your predominant theory base?
- What do you plan to do with your dissertation?

- What is your reputation among your current students?

There are certain questions that cannot be legally asked during an interview. Although committee members are informed about these, they sometimes err. Below is a list of some questions fitting this category that have been posed to your authors:

1. Are you married?

2. How is the health of your partner and child?

3. How old are you?

4. Are they still trying to get rid of Dr. Bond over there at University A (University A being your university)?

5. Why didn't your department get accredited?

Regardless of the way you are asked, these questions should not be answered, but that doesn't mean, necessarily, that you should explicitly decline to answer. Perhaps the key here is similar to all interview questions: take a little time to think about what is *really* being asked, and decide how best to respond.

EXIT INTERVIEW

The exit interview is usually conducted by either the chair of the search committee or the chair of the department. This meeting presents you with a final campus opportunity to ask questions—and you should have some, if you are at all interested in getting the position. Things that have come up during the authors' exit interviews as candidates have included: salary, compensation package, courses they wanted taught, issues within the department, their experience with the interviews, and personal reactions to certain people they met (e.g., the eccentric dean).

THANK YOU NOTES

Following your return home from each interview, you should take the time to send thank you notes to each person of significance (dean, faculty, office assistant, etc.) you met on campus. These notes should be short, should be hand-written, and should refer to something specific that transpired during the visit.

EXAMPLE (written to the department's office assistant):

Dear Ms. Jones,

I want to thank you very much for the professional courtesy you extended to me on my recent campus visit. I really appreciated when you noticed that my schedule was running tight and re-arranged my meeting time with Human Resources. Your department is obviously well served by both your competence and your insight.

Thank you,

Jon Peters

CHAPTER 5

The Negotiation

RANK ORDER THE POSITIONS

Before considering negotiation, compile a list of possible jobs, including notes on each visit (the position, the people, the place). Rank order the jobs. Truly mull over your possibilities, as this will enable you to remain grounded and focused when you receive an offer or offers.

WHAT YOU CAN NEGOTIATE

The very first thing to recognize about the negotiating process is that everything, theoretically, is on the table. Salary, rank, classification within rank (step), courses, professional development allocations, and many other items can be—and have been—negotiated, sometimes to the benefit of the applicant, sometimes the university, sometimes both. That said, each institution has unique regulations that preclude some things' being negotiated: all universities have their own ways of trimming the theoretical field to specific, practical options. For example, you may find yourself offered a position with a university that's part of a larger collective-bargaining unit (e.g., a state education system). If so, you may not be able to negotiate the rank at which you are hired (e.g., associate professor vs. assistant professor), but you may be able to start at a higher step within a given rank (e.g., step 3 instead of step 1). Such negotiations, of course, can result in a higher beginning salary.

On the other hand, if you are dealing with a university that is not part of a union, you may be able to negotiate the actual starting pay. In many cases, the administrator to whom you're talking has not begun the negotiation at the highest pay possible. Keep that in mind. The department and university have spent a lot time and effort to get to you, and have now offered you a position, so you have some leverage in this discussion.

How are negotiations conducted? Usually, the department chair or dean will call you with a job offer. Obviously, this will be an exciting moment. But you should take care not to react too quickly with a yes or no. Listen closely to the offer and ask for clarification on points that are unclear. At this juncture, it is best to thank the chair or dean and ask for some time to think about the offer. Before hanging up, determine when they need to know your answer and let them know that you may call back for further information.

There are several reasons to take your time here. You need to formulate and clarify what you will require in order to accept the position. And you need to reconsider the university, department, faculty, and students, along with any other particular variables important to you. You need to develop any questions regarding your potential job duties. Finally, as we stated earlier, you may have multiple job offers on the same day (it happened to one of this book's authors). Don't jump at the first one unless it's at the top of your list. Take whatever time is available to consider options.

If you are offered a position at University A and have been waiting to hear back from University B (which is ranked #1 on your list), you will need to call the chair of University B's search committee to let him or her know you have received an offer. It is perfectly acceptable to then ask when you should expect to hear from University B regarding the position.

During the negotiation process, we have found it of utmost importance to be honest with your potential employer (remembering that you may have a long career there). Be clear about what you feel you need if you're going to join the university—you probably won't get what you don't ask for. Be professional at all times, because, as we have indicated previously, you will be working in a subculture of a subculture of a subculture. From the start of the search to the signing of your contract (actually, even before and after these moments), make sure you do not burn any bridges or cause any negativity to fall your way. Academe is a small world. Your particular area of specialization is even smaller.

Some specific items that you might include in your negotiations are a new computer and/or resources and equipment for your research, a decreased teaching load for the first year or two, necessary technology and software for teaching, moving expenses, a return trip to look for housing, and money to attend specialized training in your field to augment your teaching and/or research.

The Sample Letter provides some ideas about how to frame your negotiations, create boundaries, and identify language useful in this process.

Sample Counter-offer Letter

May 00, 20__
Dean [Name]
Office of the Dean
University of America
PO Box 00
City B, State 00000-0000

Dear Dean [Name],

Thank you for the flattering offer to join the faculty at the University of America (U of A). I am excited about the possibility of joining the faculty, and I very much enjoyed meeting with you and your colleagues during my time on campus last week.

In reference to the offer you extended on Monday, I wanted to gather more specific information about various issues you presented, and to make some requests that might make my decision to accept the job offer a bit easier. First, I am interested in knowing the specific tenure requirements for pre-tenured faculty members at U of A. That is, what is required with regard to research, teaching, and service activities in order to ensure a successful tenure review, and what would U of A expect from a faculty member already coming in with the rank of associate professor? Moreover, given my tenure at the University of the United States (U of US), how many years of credit might I receive toward my tenure clock at U of A?

Second, in considering the startup package you offered, I found that I might need a bit more support in order to ensure a successful tenure review within the next couple of years. Along with the graduate assistant position for three years, $3,000 consulting fee, and $2,000 travel budget you indicated in the offer, I would like to request a research subsidy to cover anticipated expenses associated with (a) setting up my office (purchasing items such as a computer, scanner, printer, data analysis software, television/VCR/DVD combo burner/player for viewing student tapes, office furniture, filing cabinets, chairs, lamps, books, etc.); (b) developing my research program at U of A; and (c) traveling to professional conferences and consulting with colleagues with whom I engage in research collaborations. In light of these professional expenses, which I tie very closely to my potential success in achieving tenure at U of A, I anticipate needing $15,000-$20,000 in addition to the startup package you offered on Monday. If it would be more financially prudent to dispense the research subsidy over a period of 2-3 years, that would be fine. In addition, as you know, I am on the American Counseling Association's ballot to run for President of the Counselors for Social Justice (CSJ). If I should win the election, what types of support (e.g., administrative support or additional office space) might be available at U of A to sustain my presidency?

The salary you offered for the position at U of A is compelling, but it seems like a lateral move for me financially, in light of the upcoming cost of living, merit, and promotion increases I would obtain this fall if I were to remain at U of US. Furthermore, coming to U of A would mean sacrificing my tenured status here at U of US, which I am willing to do because of my strong interest in being a part of the Counselor Education program at U of A. Moreover, there is a fairly marked difference in the cost of living indices between the [City A, State] area and the [City B, State] area, with the [City B] cost of living being substantially higher. Therefore, I would like to request an incoming salary of between $[reasonable counter-offer].

I am traveling to South Africa this summer as a part of an Association for Multicultural Development effort to conduct outreach at the University of Botswana. I have sought a fellowship at U of US to help defray the cost of the trip and am expected to receive the fellowship. If I should announce that I am leaving U of US to go to U of A, I am certain that the fellowship funds will become null and void. Might there be fellowship support available at U of A for this trip? The estimated cost of the trip is $6,110, which includes round trip airfare from Washington, D.C., ground transportation, lodging, meals, various outreach initiatives, and a tour of historic sites and national treasures.

I also would like to inquire about the possibility of one or two of my current doctoral students at U of US transferring to U of A's Counselor Education program in the fall of 20__ or 20__. If this is possible, what kinds of support might be available to them?

Lastly, with so much going on this summer and the shortness of time between now and the August 15th start date you indicated, might there be monies available to cover my travel expenses (e.g., flight, hotel, transportation) to [City B] in the next month or two to secure a place to live?

Thank you very much for considering the issues outlined in this letter. I look forward to hearing from you soon.

Sincerely,

[Your Name]
Associate Professor
University of the United States

SECTION 2

Stories from the Field

What follows is a series of chapters authored by professionals who have all had up-close and personal experiences of the job search. Each chronicle touches, in the author's individual style, on successes and failures; you will find many of the suggestions made in the preceding material supported anecdotally.

Some themes are recurrent. The most prominent is the admonition that the applicant remain genuine during the entire process. The consensus seems to be that search committees (and the universities that empower them) are interested in the real product. Attempting to appear as someone you *think* you should be rather than clearly demonstrating who and what you really are is probably fatal to your chances.

There are also numerous exhortations to target your application materials toward the specific position for which you are applying; the "Dear Occupant" approach is clearly seen as a waste of time and money. Since many are called (see especially the contributions from the field of English) and few are chosen, your materials must stand out from the crowd.

Separate from the formal interview and presentation process, our contributors also document the immense importance of the informal interactions that occur during the campus visit. Mis-steps here (e.g., lack of handwashing, overbearing arrogance) can be disastrous, while demonstrations of flexibility (e.g., dealing with changes in the campus schedule) give the candidate the chance to shine.

So consider these unique sharings.

CHAPTER 6

Plan Ahead:
Expect the Unexpected

By Jason Willow

Filling a faculty position seems a fairly straightforward process: a university determines the need for a faculty member, the position is advertised nationally, the candidates are narrowed down to a suitable three to five for on-campus interviews, and the most qualified individual is offered and accepts the position. In an ideal world, this is precisely what would happen. Unfortunately, we don't live in an ideal world. In the following pages, I provide personal insight into the job-searching process through an intermingling of my own experiences both as a job searcher and as a search-committee member. My goal in this chapter is to help prepare the searcher for the job hunt by highlighting common mistakes made by applicants. I have also included a significant amount of "insider information" concerning the job search and, more specifically, important details that position announcements don't provide.

I write this chapter with the following assumptions. First, I will assume that you are close to completing your terminal degree, have located positions of interest, and have either begun the application process or expect to in the near future. With this assumption, I will avoid discussion of resources that are available to help locate positions. Second, I will assume that you have been properly versed in the basic tenets of preparation and organization of the curriculum vitae. Therefore, I will avoid discussion of the structural integrity of the vitae. Finally, I will assume that other sections of this text have provided a wealth of detailed information regarding the process of the job search. Hence, where I feel that I can be most helpful is in providing anecdotal, *post hoc* advice on selected topics of relevance based on my experiences both as a job searcher and as a search-committee member.

THE APPLICATION PACKET

Although cliché, at no point does the phrase "you have one chance to make a first impression" have more relevance than in the preparation of application materials for a faculty position. Your application packet must convey everything about you that makes you the ideal candidate for the job. It must also not sabotage your chances at obtaining the position of interest. From the perspective of a search committee, here is what we are looking for: attention to detail, self-promotion without egotism, and the ability to present a comprehensive snapshot of yourself in as few words as possible. With these objectives in mind, take heed of the following suggestions.

The cover letter is not going to be the deciding factor in whether or not you get the job

The cover letter in and of itself will not get you the job. There is a reason you're asked to submit an application packet: the committee wants to know as much about you as it can. When preparing the cover letter, you should be brief. Express your interest in the position, describe how you came to know of the position, describe your qualifications, and detail what you've enclosed in the application packet. As a general rule, one page is sufficient—most search-committee members will not read beyond the first few paragraphs. I once had an English professor assign a five to seven page descriptive essay on a topic of choice. On the day the paper was due, she told the class to revise the paper into three pages without damaging its meaning. What seemed extraordinarily difficult at the time resulted in a much stronger, more focused final submission. There is nothing that you can say in two pages of a cover letter that couldn't be said in one. If you are finding it difficult to revise to a single page, you are going into too much detail.

The cover letter might just be the deciding factor in whether or not you get the job

While it is true that the cover letter alone won't get you the job, it may be a significant factor in your getting turned down. Three words: grammar, spelling, details. I know the drill: check the *Chronicle*, make a list of positions available, adapt your stock cover-letter to each position, copy your vitae and associated application materials, and send the packets off in the mail. However, before you seal the envelope, check your spelling, check your grammar, and check the details. Have someone read the letter before you send it, as errors are often missed simply because the document has become too familiar to the author. As a search-committee member, I have more than once reviewed cover letters addressed to an entirely different school. This creates a doubly bad situation, because if I am receiving a cover letter addressed to a different school, it might mean that the other school is reading the cover letter that should have come to me. The applicant may have just cost him- or herself not one, but two jobs. Now granted, the search committee will still review your materials, but it makes a poor first impression. It suggests that you are not detail-oriented. I have heard in committee, "How interested in this position is this person if they did not take the time to check their application packet for errors?" Two minutes of proofreading may be the difference between an on-campus interview and a "there were many qualified applicants" letter.

The vitae shows how you are different from your counterparts

Vitae is defined as "a *brief* resume of one's *career and training*, as prepared by a person applying for a job." I have highlighted the most relevant aspects of the definition. The vitae should be as brief as possible, while presenting you adequately, and it should focus on your career and training, as they relate to the position of interest. Figuratively speaking, you are going to be thrown into a pile of candidates, each of whom feels that he or she is the most suited for the position advertised. Your vitae and cover letter are tools used not only to inform the search committee of your qualifications, but to market yourself as the most qualified candidate. In doing so, however, you should avoid wasting a lot of time and space detailing experiences that are irrelevant to the current position. Perhaps your position at the local Whippy Dip as a junior in high school allowed you to get that 1985 Chevy Cavalier that you had your eye on, but did that experience make you a better candidate for a faculty position? Probably not. That said, the vitae is a vital source of information that will be the primary reference for conveying information about who you are. The following suggestions are offered with that in mind.

Make yourself different from your peers

From a search committee's perspective, while it's quite easy to narrow your pool down to ten, it's sometimes nearly impossible to move from ten to three without having a horrible, sinking feeling that someone between numbers four and ten was "the one." As a searcher, you must find a way to distinguish yourself from your colleagues. During a recent search, I had four applicants from the same academic program at a nearby university. All were either just finished with or about to finish their terminal degrees, all had nearly identical teaching and service experiences, and the reference lists could have been photocopies. There was nothing that distinguished one individual from the next, and it is my opinion that this was detrimental to each applicant's candidacy. Find experiences that distinguish you from your peers, especially if you will be applying for positions with colleagues from your graduate program.

Don't embellish minor accomplishments

Remember, the vitae is "a brief resume of one's career and training," not a work of fiction. If you were the teaching assistant for a course and your responsibilities were entering grades into an excel sheet for the professor, you probably are not safe listing it as a teaching experience. There is an excellent chance that you will be asked to give a sample lecture if you are invited to campus; save yourself the embarrassment of having to teach a topic beyond your level of comfort.

It's what you have done, not what you are planning to do

A common practice I have encountered in admission packets, especially when it comes to junior faculty and newly conferred PhDs, is including citations of scholarly work "in progress." The vitae should be used to describe what you have done, not what you plan on doing. If my school recognized all the scholarly activities I have considered undertaking, I would have received tenure moments after setting my first foot on campus. Activities that have been completed, have been peer-reviewed, and have been communicated are vitae-worthy; current projects and plans can be detailed in the research statement.

THE PHONE INTERVIEW

If you have made the first cut, the next step is most likely the phone interview. This is the only time in the entire process where you may be able to change the impression formed on the basis of your application packet. This can be a good thing. Unfortunately, it can also be a disaster, if you're not prepared.

The phone interview is your first opportunity to present your personality. It is also your opportunity to show that you have done your homework and have not sent your application materials merely because the position was advertised (even though that may be the case). A sucessful football coach once observed that when a football team passes the ball, three things can happen and two of them are bad. The team could throw a completion, which is good, or they could either throw an incompletion or an interception, both bad. Similarly, when you have a phone interview, three things can happen, but in this case only one of them is bad. You can garner support for a strong application packet—good. You can improve your candidacy by enhancing a relatively weak application packet—also good. And you can sabotage a strong application packet with a poor interview—bad. Below, I focus on when good goes bad in the hope of helping you to avoid it.

Do your homework

Prior to the interview, you should gather as much information about the school as possible. Read and understand its mission statement. Familiarize yourself with the faculty members in the program to which you are applying (hint: many of them are likely to be in the room during the interview). Investigate other programs at the university as well; search committees love to hear about the possibility of interdisciplinary work, so your ability to find opportunities for collaboration outside the program is likely to be looked upon favorably.

As a professor, I have always loved the student who comes to the office to ask for extra credit and offers the following story: "Dr. Willow, I don't understand it, I was up all night studying for this exam. I can't understand how I got a 12%." Just as you would not recommend that your students cram for an exam, you should not cram for a phone interview. And do not bring a cheat sheet. I once interviewed an individual who, as became obvious after approximately five minutes of questions, interviewed while sitting at his computer. How did we know? We heard mouse clicks when we asked questions about the individual's knowledge of our university. "Can you tell us how your teaching philosophy complements the mission of Gannon University?" [click, click, click] "Sure, I feel that . . ." What followed was an extended period of fragmented sentences while the candidate read the mission statement and tried to formulate an answer. If you are being interviewed, you can safely assume that the committee expects you to be able to read, do your homework, and go beyond the "about us" section of the university website.

It's not what you say, it's how you say it

Confident, controlled, and concise: these are words of wisdom when preparing for your phone interview. Do not think that because you are a decent public speaker you do not have to prepare yourself to be interviewed. A common and often fatal flaw is deciding to "wing it" and let the vitae speak for itself. This overconfidence is often reflected in a candidate's inability to answer questions effectively—in essence, saying a lot about nothing.

Nervousness frequently produces the same effect, manifesting in the tendency to go on and on. If you have served as an instructor in any capacity, you can recognize students who do not know the answer to a question. Rather than leave the question blank, they write everything they *do* know in the hope of getting partial credit based on quantity alone. When we get nervous during the phone interview, especially while trying to make sense of questions or formulate our answers, we tend to begin a mental dialogue and put our verbalization on autopilot. If you can feel that happening, ask for the question to be reiterated, ask for clarification, ask if you have answered accordingly—just don't get caught in a maze of non-answers.

The same strategy can help you avoid awkward silences. In a recent search, there was a consistent eight to ten second pause after each question as the candidate pondered an answer. After first questioning the quality of our connection, the committee became rather annoyed. That is not a mood that you would prefer in a search committee. Repeating the question aloud and/or asking for clarification before answering gives you an opportunity to formulate your answer while avoiding "dead air."

THE ON-CAMPUS INTERVIEW

I will not spend a great deal of time discussing the on-campus interview, but rather just give a couple of insider tips. You should understand that at this point in the process, the committee, while maintaining the public stance of openness, has its favorite. There is not a lot that is going to change its collective mind. Hopefully, you are that favorite. The possibility exists, however, that you are a sacrificial lamb brought on campus so that the committee can demonstrate to the provost or president that it has been diligent in its search.

That being said, a few brief comments: although one hopes it will not hold sway over the decision-making process, you *will* be judged on how you dress, you *will* be judged on your table manners, you *will* be judged on your eye contact during conversation, and you *will* be judged on the firmness of your handshake (men and women alike). Suffice it to say that nearly all of your actions *will* be judged. I once saw a candidate for a dean's position all but eliminate himself from contention by casually joking that he "craved power." The committee provided ample opportunity for the candidate to lessen the scope of the statement, which he did, but its bitter taste lingered, and the comment resurfaced during post-interview discussion.

Think of a snow globe, ever popular during the holiday season. Picture the globe containing a little village and a miniature figure. That miniature figure is you during an on-campus interview. Good luck.

THE AFTER PARTY

After you have interviewed, it is good practice to formally thank the search-committee chair and committee members for taking the time to meet with you. Regardless of whether you are offered the position, you would like to leave the process on good terms, for two reasons. First, there may be an opening at the school in the future. Second, search-committee members have friends at other schools in which you may have an interest, so a good impression can extend beyond the university walls.

Because I have had my own encounters with professional rejection, I have added a few more comments below. They bear an important message: "Do not burn your bridges . . . unless warranted."

Don't take it personally if you don't get offered the position

Take a moment and think about all your friends and colleagues who are in a position similar to yours: finishing your degree, preparing application packet after application packet, and waiting for a call from anyone offering to bring you to a campus for an interview. You are not alone. I have never served on a search committee that saw fewer than fifty applications for a single position. Often times, several of the applicants were more than qualified. Unfortunately, only one individual is ever offered the position, meaning that at least forty-nine people always get the "many qualified applicants" letter. You may already be starting your collection. I would be lying if I denied possessing an envelope containing over thirty such letters, all accumulated during my own search. It is important to keep the job search in perspective.

Search committees have limited information with which to make their decision, so of course they will not be able to get a comprehensive picture of who you are. Often, who we are on paper is very different from who we are in person. It is only natural to feel slighted when turned down. We all believe that we are more than capable in our occupational pursuits—so why didn't the search committee see how much potential you have? Don't take it personally, and don't burn bridges or hold grudges after being rejected. I recently hired an individual for an assistant-professor position whom I had declined to interview eleven months earlier, when he first applied for the same position. As is sometimes the case, the individual originally hired left the university after only two semesters, and the position was open again. The individual to whom I offered it accepted graciously. Had he taken exception to not being interviewed the first time though, the current opportunity might not have presented itself. With that in mind . . .

Sometimes, it is okay to take it personally when you don't get offered a position

In January of 2002, I applied for a position at my undergraduate alma mater. The description looked as if it had been written based on my vitae. I pursued it aggressively, but received very little feedback for several months. I contacted Human Resources a number of times and was told that the search "was ongoing." Several weeks later, after an additional call to Human Resources, I was told that the position had been filled. Several weeks after this, I received the "there were many qualified applicants letter" in the mail. Now, it is important to note two significant pieces of information: first, this was my undergraduate alma mater in the town in which I grew up; second, the year was 2002. The rejection letter I received had two alarming mistakes. It was addressed to "Mr. Williams"—though I had been a Dr. for several months and a Willow for 31 years—and it was dated 1999—three years before I applied. Granted, this was an obvious clerical error, and I later received an additional letter with the previous errors corrected, but since this was my alma mater, yes, I took it personally.

THINGS THEY DON'T TELL YOU IN THE JOB DESCRIPTION

Finally, I would like to shed light on some issues that you're not likely to know unless you have been through the process. Just a few odds and ends to keep in mind as you begin or continue your search.

Sometimes the position mysteriously goes away

It is not unheard of to go through the entire application process, spend time on campus during an interview, perhaps even get offered the position, and then find that the position has mysteriously disappeared. This is especially true when applying for positions at private institutions. Most private schools are enrollment-driven, which means that financial decisions and, unfortunately, new faculty positions, depend upon the school meeting budgetary projections. If enrollment projections fall short of expectations, belts are tightened and budgetary cuts have to be made. What was once a new hire becomes an open but unfilled faculty line. It doesn't happen a lot, but you should know that it is a possibility so you that are not surprised if it does.

Beware the internal candidate

True story: I was invited to a relatively large campus in the Midwest for an interview. I arrived the night before and met with the search committee for dinner. I felt an immediate connection to the committee and the program, to the point of calling my fiancé that evening and saying, "I would be shocked if I don't get this job." The next day I toured the campus, the department, and related facilities. I gave a guest lecture and had a lively interaction with the students in the class. Again, I felt a strong connection: this school felt like home. I was getting excellent vibes from the search-committee chair, who shared stories about his family and personal interests beyond what would be expected on a formal job interview.

Then, approximately fifteen minutes prior to my leaving campus, the search chair introduced me to a graduate student in the program. "This is Dr. Jason Willow," he said. "He's an applicant for the assistant professor position in sport and exercise psychology." "Oh," said the graduate student, with a mild amount of surprise. "I thought that was Alan's position." In a matter of eight seconds, I knew that I would not be getting the job, that I had fallen victim to a monster so ferocious that it makes grown men whimper: the dreaded internal candidate.

If I had to estimate, I would say that approximately 25 to 30 percent of the positions advertised nationally have already been given to an internal candidate. It is the nature of the academic game. Again, this says nothing about you as a candidate; you had no chance from the start. Interestingly, I contacted the above-mentioned committee chair after receiving my "many qualified candidates" letter to ask what I, as a job seeker, could do differently in my next interview to increase my chances of being hired. The chair's response was particularly telling: "Honestly ... nothing. The committee liked you very much, and was somewhat disappointed that we didn't have two positions to offer."

I will shortly begin conducting a search in my very own program. There is a 99.9 percent chance that the position will be offered to the individual who is currently filling the line as a temporary faculty member. Is it fair? It doesn't seem so for the applicants who are not aware of the internal candidate, but again, this is how the game works. Sometimes, the game is not fair.

A FINAL WORD

Again, I offer this chapter not as a how-to manual for obtaining a position in academia, but as a collection of snapshots of my experiences in the search process. In my efforts to obtain employment, I came up against injustices. In my role as a search-committee member, I have seen what has worked and what has failed. I hope the above comments shed some light on the process and help you along the way as you attempt to enter the workforce.

Jason Willow, PhD
Assistant Professor and Program Coordinator
Sports and Exercise Science, Gannon University

CHAPTER 7

Persistence:
Conducting a Successful Search
in a Tough Market

By Bradley Will

PhD candidates often have the mistaken notion that, having paid their dues and served their time as graduate students, they will land solid, tenure-track jobs shortly after or even before completing their dissertations. I know I thought so. While many PhD candidates have just such a future in store, others are less likely to achieve success—regardless of their standings as graduate students. Any job search is affected by market forces external to the job seeker. For academic jobs, these forces differ among disciplines, and in some cases, the job market for a given discipline can be tilted dramatically against job seekers.

I am most familiar with the job market in my own discipline—English. Ten years ago, the Modern Language Association—the dominant professional association in English and foreign-language academia—conducted a survey of the number of new PhDs granted and the number of academic jobs available during the 1996–97 academic year. The findings were grim, and not surprising for those of us on the job market at the time. Conspicuously, neither the MLA nor any other organization in English has updated these statistics, but even though the data are more than ten years old, they still present a good general sense of the current job market in English. In 1996–97 there were 1,817 new PhDs granted in English. That same year, 670 tenure-track positions were filled in the discipline. This reflects an employment rate of only 37%. Full-time, non-tenure-track jobs accounted for an additional 460 positions filled.

Those numbers are dismal. Slightly more than a third of the people earning PhDs in English in 1997 found full-time, tenure-track employment. We might assume that those who had renewable, non-tenure-track appointments were satisfied with their employment status, but this increases the percentage of successful job seekers to only 62%. This is an obvious disconnect between supply and demand. The supply of PhDs (1,817) was ridiculously high when compared to the demand for people to fill full-time academic jobs in English (1,130). Far too many people were competing for a small number of jobs. The discipline granted 1,817 PhDs, but only opened full-time jobs for 1,130.

Actually, the truth of the market is even worse. The MLA survey ignores a large segment of job seekers. Those 1,817 new PhDs in English were not the only ones on the job market. We must remember to add the unknown number of unsuccessful 1995–96 PhDs to the supply of 1996–97 PhDs, since previous years' unsuccessful PhDs and even some PhDs with established careers were seeking jobs again. In fact, we can surmise from the data above that the supply of PhDs from the following year, 1997–98, was increased by 687 unemployed and underemployed PhDs from 1996–97. The carryover from year to year becomes nightmarish. Those 687 unemployed and underemployed PhDs were likely back on the job market, competing against approximately 1,800 new PhDs for the usual small number of jobs.

So what should the academic job seeker learn from this? First and foremost, you should research and understand the job market in your discipline. Find out how supply and demand stack up in your field. Find out the number of PhD's recently granted in your discipline. Survey the past year's advertisements in the *Chronicle of Higher Education* (or a similar publication) to determine the number of full-time tenure-track and non-tenure track jobs available over the last year. You might find that the supply of PhDs in your field cannot keep up with the demand—as is currently the case for PhDs in business. There is an increased demand for professors of business, while fewer people are pursuing PhDs in business, preferring instead to avoid the cost of graduate school in favor of the higher earning potential that an MBA or undergraduate degree brings. If you are lucky enough to be in such a sellers' market, with low supply and high demand, then you can be confident in the success of your job search.

However, if you find that your discipline has a high supply of PhDs and a low demand for full-time academicians, then you must recognize that you will face a highly competitive job market with an uncertain outcome and a real possibility of failure. Pursuing employment in a glutted job market requires that you accept some unpleasant propositions, but planning for such a market can increase the likelihood of success. You can expect that more job listings will require applicants to have already completed their dissertations, so you might direct your energy more toward finishing your degree than finding a job. You will be less able to select the region in which you will be employed, so you might consider broadening your search to a national or international scale; working in a region that is far too cold, far too hot, far too urban, or far too rural for your taste is still preferable to not working at all.

Additionally, if you are in a high-supply, low-demand market, you will be less likely to land a job at a research-oriented institution, so you might plan to teach, emphasizing pedagogy classes in your coursework and loading your letters of recommendation to reflect your teaching ability. Teaching four (or even five) large undergraduate classes each semester may seem like a high workload, but a high workload is far and away preferable to having no workload at all. In short, job seekers who find that they are part of a glut of new PhDs will probably need to reassess their expectations and be more open to jobs that they otherwise might not have accepted, or even applied for.

If you have done the research and know in advance that your market is weighted even slightly toward a high supply of PhDs, you can adjust your expectations and your search strategies immediately, in your first season on the job market. You will thereby increase dramatically your chances of not needing to go on the market for a second, third, or fourth season. Job seekers unaware of market forces working against them are unlikely to land the dream positions on which they're so tightly focused. Their initial job searches will probably end in failure. Remember that 63% of those 1996–97 English PhDs did not get full-time, tenure-track jobs. Those who have not researched the market will not learn that it is glutted until their first job searches fail. Having received those all-too-real rejection letters stating that theirs were one of four- or five- or six-hundred applications for a single position, they will realize that they need to adjust their strategies for the next season—but by that time they may have lost months or even a year on a search that was too narrowly delineated.

Seekers in a glutted market should seriously consider accepting an offer of part-time or temporary academic employment. Such work—while usually difficult, underpaid, and impermanent—is an opportunity to build your CV and strengthen your application. In addition to keeping your foot in the academic door, part-time or temporary employment gives you the chance to demonstrate your ability as a teacher and a colleague, rather than as a graduate student. Most members of search committees are well aware that the attributes that make an outstanding graduate student do not necessarily make an outstanding professor. An application letter that explains how you have successfully maintained a four-four teaching load is more impressive than an application letter that describes how you graded another professor's essays as part of a teaching assistantship.

I earned my PhD in English in 1998, in the midst of a glutted market that, ten years later, shows little sign of changing. I expected to work at a teaching institution, so I supplemented my study of American literature with coursework in teaching first-year composition (the bread-and-butter course of most U.S. English departments). I went on the market well before I completed my dissertation, and I declined an offer of temporary appointment at a community college where I had interviewed for a full-time, tenure-track position. About one year after completing my PhD, I again received an offer of temporary appointment after interviewing for a full-time, tenure-track position—this time at a small, teaching-oriented state university. I accepted this position, knowing there was a strong possibility that another full-time, tenure-track position would be available in this department the following semester.

That first semester, my title was "Visiting Assistant Professor," but I behaved as if I were on a sixteen-week job interview. I heeded the advice of my dissertation director: "If you want this to turn into a tenure-track appointment, you have to make yourself indispensable." I took every opportunity to demonstrate my expertise, energy, and willingness to take on extra tasks. I created a web page for the department (back when many departments had no web presence) and became the indispensable web master. The department brought in candidates for that full-time, tenure-track position, and I interviewed for the position, too. No one handed me that tenure-track position; I was the best, strongest candidate interviewed. I have since been tenured and promoted, and I moved on from webmaster to Director of Composition.

My job search was successful. I beat the odds when the market was heavily stacked against me. I attribute my success to planning, persistence, and hard work, but I know that glutted job markets leave many PhDs without employment in their chosen fields. Planning, persistence, and hard work do not always pay off, and many potential stars never get the opportunity to shine.

Bradley Will, PhD
Associate Professor of English and Assistant Dean of Arts and Sciences, English Department, Fort Hays State University

CHAPTER 8

The Old Dog Learns a New Trick: Academia's Research-Faculty Track

By Darin J. Knapp

The traditional career track for those seeking to be university or college professors, or academic scientists, is the tenure track. Having academic tenure means holding a faculty position more or less permanently, without periodic contract renewals or associated reviews. Gaining academic tenure requires earning the degrees and undertaking research appropriate to the tenure candidate's field of study, doing extensive preparatory work, submitting appropriate application materials, identifying supporters, networking, and lecturing, among other activities. The tenure candidate should expect to compete for the job in every way conceivable. Landing a tenure-track job is just the beginning of the process of gaining tenure. The candidate for tenure strives to continue to excel at research and/or teaching and scholarship while working toward promotion to tenured status, a process described from various perspectives elsewhere in this book.

What about the person who wants to be a university or college professor or an academic scientist, but for whom the traditional tenure track is either unavailable or unattractive? This person might consider the research track, an academic alternative to the tenure track that is particularly relevant to careers oriented toward scientific and biomedical research. The research track in academia is growing in popularity, utility, and importance. According to the 2006 Contingent Faculty Index, compiled by the American Association of University Professors, nearly 15,000 full-time research faculty across the country were on the research track as of Fall 2005. Most were working at doctoral and research universities. The rate of growth in research-track jobs exceeds that of tenure-track jobs. Together, research-track and non-tenure, teaching-track faculty comprise more than 65% of all full-time faculty at 2,600 institutions across the country.

While the research track is associated with many of the same opportunities and responsibilities as the tenure track, the tracks differ in some fundamental ways. The aspiring academic should be aware of the research track as a potential career path and should understand how it compares to the tenure track. This chapter discusses research-track positions and considers differences between research-track and tenure-track paths with the intention of enhancing academic job seekers' awareness of options besides the traditional tenure-track path.

The research-track position evolved, in part, from the recognition by universities of the need to offer diverse faculty positions and work opportunities in order to remain nationally and internationally competitive. Moreover, universities recognize that positions dedicated to full-time research (with little or no formal teaching responsibility) can be integral to furthering institutional research missions. While tenure *per se* is not part of the research track, universities increasingly employ research-oriented faculty with titles of assistant professor, associate professor, or professor as appropriate. This practice arose partly from the concern that classifying research-track positions as non-faculty positions with titles such as "research scientist" or "engineer" might compromise success in obtaining external grant funding.

While research-track faculty spend the majority of their time conducting research and securing research funding, they also fulfill other functions: serving on various university and departmental committees; participating in the faculty governance process; serving as principal investigators on independent, externally funded research; and, often, teaching. The teaching aspect generally entails supervising and advising graduate students and postdocs in their research endeavors. Departmental lectures and select classroom initiatives are not uncommon. Considerable variety exists across research-track endeavors. This variety not only blurs the line between the research and tenure tracks, but also appears to provide flexibility for both the faculty and the university in furthering their respective goals.

Searching for a research-track position and developing a strategy for getting job interviews can involve much the same work and activities needed to secure a tenure-track position. However, one job-search strategy that applies more often to the research track than the tenure track is seeking such a position from the inside—that is, at the aspiring research-track candidate's current institution. For example, the research-track candidate might progress from a postdoctoral position at a university to either a research associate or, more directly, to a research-track assistant professor at the same university. The tenure-track job, on the other hand, is almost always sought and offered at an institution other than the candidate's current institution. For the research-track candidate, seeking a position from the inside entails concurrently securing a university commitment and, typically, a grant that can support the candidate's salary and research. This effort requires review and support from a department relevant to the candidate's research endeavors, and a senior investigator willing to collaborate with the candidate on a research effort.

Funding of the research-track position is probably one of the most important distinguishing features of this career option. Self-funding through grants, rather than direct department-level support, is the norm. Tenure-track jobs, on the other hand, are typically funded through department-level support. However, the lines between the tenure track and the research track blur here. Some departments provide limited direct support for their tenured faculty, and great pressure exists to maintain self-funding through grants—a situation similar to that of the research track.

Another feature of the research track that can be considered here is the relative opportunity to build a reputation. The bottom line is that a researcher's reputation is built largely on quality research regardless of whether the researcher is on the tenure track or the research track. A national and international reputation can be built on either track, based on hard work and discovery. Researchers on tenure or research tracks can publish in the best journals as long as the work they do is novel and important.

How does one secure a research-track position? A typical scenario looks like this: Complete your advanced degree (typically a scientific one) and seek a postdoctoral position in research at a major university. This postdoctoral search may take you far afield, and is similar in some key respects to the tenure-track or research-track job search that would start during your final postdoctoral year. That is, the application and resume-preparation, the job interview, research presentation, and interviews with department faculty and staff are all part of this postdoctoral research-position search.

Once you have gotten the job and spend at least a year or two aggressively pursuing the research plan that you and your senior mentor develop, you reach a choice point in your career: do I stay or do I go? This decision can be difficult because the considerations at play can push you in both directions at the same time. On the traditional career path, this is the time when you apply for the tenure-track positions. Depending on your desires, previous success, abilities, and a fair amount of luck, you compete with fifty to two hundred or more other candidates for a single tenure-track job.

On the non-traditional academic career path, this is a time to entertain a range of questions, such as "Do I like where I am now?" "Am I at a great university now?" "Do I like my colleagues and the intellectual environment where I am now?" "Does my institution have a consistent and fair track record of promoting research-based faculty?" "Do I have opportunities to do the research that I want to do here, or would I be best served by going somewhere else?" "Are other professional career advancement options even available where I am now?" The answers do not necessarily come easily, and the advice of those on the research or tenure tracks may not necessarily hold the answer that is best for you. Other questions that you might entertain: "Does my significant other have a good job/career path where he or she is now?" (This critical question is also asked while considering the tenure-track job search.) The culmination of this job search can mean that a partner gives up his or her existing job for something less attractive in the new locale. Sometimes the successful tenure-track job seeker's new department will aggressively "shake the tree" for the job seeker's partner during the interview/review process and find a job at the same university for the partner. Of course, these efforts are not always successful.

Careful thought brings out still other critical issues. If the aspiring academic has children, he or she must ask, "What is the quality of the school system? Are they in an enriched environment overall?" Regardless of whether you yourself have children, other important issues about the quality of community life and the opportunities to explore fulfilling pursuits outside of work should be considered. As for this author, whose home town is Chapel Hill, North Carolina, there is a particular joy in recharging the research batteries by playing in or listening to myriad bands in the rich local-music scene, attending plays put on by top-notch performers and artists, hosting musical events, gardening, landscaping, and more. As far as salaries are concerned, you could ask, "Do I want a higher salary at the North Pole, with great ice-fishing, or a lower salary and a quality of life enriched by the arts, culture, myriad professional and collaborative opportunities, plenty of independence, and a collegial and interactive group of fellow academics?" To each her own. Regardless of your choices, there will be compromises. Best to just get to it.

Another angle from which to view financial considerations is a thorough assessment of the cost of living where your "ideal" academic position might be. It's fair to say that many an aspiring academic is late to the table on this one. Take the example of a biomedical researcher who finds herself in an inordinately expensive place like San Francisco and, understandably, feels pressure to move east. Here we have a new (or not so new) faculty member or postdoc who may have sold a house in San Francisco (if she could ever afford one there in the first place), bought a house on the East Coast that's twice as large, and banked the rest.

Having grown up in rural Pennsylvania, where the cost of living was quite low, and lived for five years in New Jersey, where the cost of living was fairly high, the issue was salient when it came time for this author to consider where to pursue the next phase of his academic/research life. While searching for a postdoctoral position in academia, it became increasingly clear that putting down roots in the pharmaceutical industry for one spouse was not necessarily 100% compatible with a postdoctoral endeavor for the other spouse. Thus, efforts to match up goals and desires had to be made, which meant considerations about income, cost of living, where to work, where to live, what to do outside of work, and so on. A number of interesting opportunities were turned down in favor of arrangements in Chapel Hill and the Research Triangle Park, North Carolina. It could be added here that having piled many of life's big events into one year (getting a PhD, landing a new job, moving to a new state, buying a house, getting married), this author would strongly recommend spacing them, if possible.

Some aspiring academics choose the small college over the large university. This option can be very attractive, especially when, for example, the aspiring academic becomes one of a small group of valued researchers or becomes involved in the startup of a new department or curriculum. Opportunities such as these may be greater at the small college than the large university. The opportunity for visibility might also be greater; the aspiring academic might take advantage of the chance to be a big fish in a small pond.

Some aspiring academics also consider future opportunities for blending academia and business—or, more specifically, academia and entrepreneurship. If entrepreneurial interests are on the table, then it's worth noting that opportunities exist, particularly in metropolitan areas with many universities and biotechnology centers, to consider consulting and academic/business initiatives (e.g., starting your own company based on the research you do). These options are not the sole province of the tenure-track academic or non-academic.

The tenure track has long been, and is likely to always be, a valid/viable structure for the academic career. In fact, it remains a centerpiece of the academic world. The intellectual stimulation, professional opportunities, joys of scientific discovery, thrill of reaching a young mind through teaching and mentoring efforts, and the general academic life offered by this track can add up to a meaningful and worthy life's endeavor. The research track offers many of the same opportunities, but has a flavor of its own that's worth a serious look. This alternate path is a growing option for the aspiring academic. While not all departments and academic institutions provide this option, more and more do. In fact, the diversity of opportunities available to the aspiring academic is richer now than ever before. While making a decision, don't be afraid to think outside the box. Fifteen thousand research-track faculty across the country have done so, so you will be in good company.

Darin J. Knapp, PhD
Associate Professor, Psychiatry Department
University of North Carolina School of Medicine

CHAPTER 9

A Single Parent's Perspective

By Susan L. Hegel

Being a single parent adds a few twists and turns to the academic search process. Not unlike a job seeker in a dual-parent family, I considered my professional and personal needs as well as my child's needs. I spent a few months considering what was essential and therefore non-negotiable, and what was desired but not required. What I realized over time surprised me, as very little on my list was job related. Almost all of my essential items were support related. If I was job hunting now, my list of essentials would be very different, since my needs and my family's needs have changed over time.

When I finished my doctoral degree at forty-one, I was living on the West Coast, far from my family in the Midwest, and had an eight-year-old son, a dog and a cat, and no home (sold in part to fund my doctoral studies). My ex-husband was under hospice care for a terminal illness. Very soon I would become my son's only parent.

Professionally, my strengths were in teaching and in clinical skill development. While I enjoyed the research process and presented frequently at conferences, the time-intensive aspect of writing/publishing was challenging. Based on these factors, I generated the following list of needs:

1. Support system for my son and me through my ex-husband's impending death.

2. Stable male role models for my son as he entered adolescence and adulthood.

3. Community where housing was affordable on only one income.

4. Community with a reputable school district.

5. Community where I could live close to work to minimize time spent commuting, thereby increasing my at-home/parenting time.

6. Position that would value my teaching and clinical expertise without stressful demands for frequent publications.

Once my needs were identified, my approach to the job search changed significantly. Though I loved living on the West Coast, I realized it was time to move. Housing prices were escalating rapidly, especially in communities with institutions of higher education. I simply could not afford to live on the West Coast on one income if I planned to purchase a home.

I decided to move closer to my family. They would be able to help with childcare when I needed to travel (e.g., for conferences). Plus, being closer to my father and brother-in-law would provide my son with stable and dependable male role models. With my parents in Michigan and my sister's family in Syracuse, I decided to limit my search to the Ohio Valley and Western New York. By this time I had eliminated all R-1 institutions from my list. I was looking for an institution that valued quality teaching and clinical skill development over research and publications.

Community specifics were the next issue on my list. I needed a community with a good school district and affordable housing. This was much more of a challenge than I expected. Before I responded to a job posting, I tried to investigate the housing costs and educational reputation of the community. At a job fair where I had a number of interviews arranged, my first question was about the cost of a starter home in the community, rather than about the position itself. When one potential employer responded that I could probably find "an upper-floor flat for about $300,000," I politely thanked her and ended the interview. A phone interview with a large university in Ohio was going very well until I asked about housing. None of the faculty lived in the city near the university; they all lived in the surrounding suburbs and commuted an hour each way. Though the job was wonderful, I withdrew my application. I needed to spend my non-working time with my son, not commuting long distances. If he had been older, perhaps my decision would have been different.

By choice, I sought out and accepted a tenure-track position at a small teaching university in northwestern Pennsylvania. The town's public school system is strong and the Friday night high school football games are well attended by the community. There truly is a village here; I hear about it promptly when my son does something less than stellar. I live in my own home on a nice lake on one paycheck, an easy 15-minute walk from campus. Sounds idyllic, right? Not always.

Teaching done right at any institution is very hard work. Lecture prep, advising, research, meetings, committee work, grading, tenure packets, conference presentations, publishing, and promotion applications can and do create stress. Time, especially for single parents, is a limited commodity, so finding a work/family balance that fits your needs is important. Identify your strengths and work hard in those areas. To do so, be willing to expect less of yourself in other areas. On good days I am able to leave my job-stress at the office so I can be a present and joyful parent at home. May you find your family/work/life balance early in your promising career.

Susan L. Hegel, PhD, CCC-SLP
Assistant Professor
Edinboro University of Pennsylvania

CHAPTER 10

Finding My Place

By Jill M. Schultz

My partner and I were looking for academic positions at approximately the same time and within the local area, close to our network of friends and family. I concentrated predominantly on the faculty listings in the *Chronicle of Higher Education*. At the time of this search I was ABD, so I was excluded from many positions that fit the radius criteria.

I self-selected out of a position with a highly regarded private liberal-arts college that invited PhDs and ABDs. The institution was seeking someone with the exact program of study I was completing. In that case my own internal negative judge determined that the college would never hire me. The decision to select myself out of the search, rather than give it my all and let the committee make the determination, continues to haunt me.

At about the same time, I found an advertised position at a local community college. I procrastinated on writing the application. In retrospect, I suspect I was conflicted about whether I would be a good fit with the institution. Although I thought I was not good enough to teach at a private liberal-arts college, I worried that I would not find stimulation and growth in a community college that was experiencing the challenges of transforming with the surrounding environment from a rural to a suburban setting. I lived in close proximity to major cities for most of my life and I wondered about my own culture shock and adjustment if I was offered the position. However, in contrast to the private college, I worried a great deal less about my perceived qualifications.

Two days before the application deadline for the community college position I received a long-distance telephone call. My grandfather had suffered a heart attack and was hospitalized. All of my priorities shuffled and I hurriedly left town. When calling home from the hospital after my grandfather had stabilized, I remembered the pending application deadline. Speaking from a payphone in the hospital cafeteria to my partner at home at her keyboard we spontaneously engineered a truly collaborative approach to applying for a faculty position. Over the sounds of hospital staff on their lunch break and the tired, worried sounds of families, I dictated a cover letter for my application. She printed the letter and a copy of my resume and shepherded my complete application to the post office.

I was invited to interview with the search committee at the community college. I spent a great deal of time reflecting on how I would cover answers relating to my professional priorities. The salary, office space, and classroom technology were of obvious importance, but I wanted to get a sense about other, equally important issues. I was particularly concerned about the campus climate in regard to sexuality and race. In my research about the institution I learned that the campus had recently adopted domestic partner benefits for all employees. This was a surprise to me as I knew that the college faculty, staff, and student body were primarily rural, White, and conservative. In fact, the stigma of an active chapter of the local KKK permeated the county's reputation. I needed to figure out during my day on campus if the college policy change was a symbol of the deep values of the college, a beacon leading the community toward enlightened change, or if this change was administrative and marginal, leaving intact an unwelcoming or suspicious environment. Similarly, I was very concerned that since I was a White applicant, the committee would assume that I shared what I perceived to be the dominant racial attitudes of the broader community.

It turned out that I was able to use my teaching demonstration to uncover partial answers to my questions. Prior to my arrival on campus I was told to prepare a teaching demonstration based on an article. I was pleased with the standardization (same article to every candidate) and prepared an activity that involved high levels of student involvement. I assumed that since this was a faculty teaching position I would be teaching a class or at least a small group of students.

I was momentarily taken aback when the chair of the five-member faculty committee stopped asking the standardized interview questions and requested that I proceed with my teaching demonstration. There were only the six of us. I made rapid mental adjustments to my demonstration as it became clear that the teaching demonstration I had prepared for 10-15 students was to be taught to five faculty members. The assigned article was on teaching philosophies and, as we all know, teaching philosophies reveal our ideas about people, knowledge, and human capacity. I had most of my questions about the viewpoints of the faculty in regard to race and sexuality—and a host of other issues—satisfactorily answered in that portion of the interview.

From that experience I was able to think more about how I might or might not fit in during that stage of the college's evolution and growth. However, one thing was clearly communicated to me by the committee and echoed something I sensed myself: the students would certainly benefit from the different experiences and perspective that I would bring into the faculty. From that strong impression I gave more weight to the consideration that I might be "good for the students."

Later, at home, my concerns shifted in a new direction. I felt some unease and confusion about the exact expectations associated with the position. The questions in the interview did not seem to be in alignment with the qualifications advertised in the job announcement. It was clear that on some level the position was still under construction. I allowed myself to conclude, perhaps prematurely, that the exact nature of the position would take shape over time, according to the intersections of my strengths and the institution's needs, and would be premised on the spirit of trust and cooperation between those who hire and those who are hired. This was, in retrospect, very naïve.

SEARCH COMMITTEE MEMBER (THREE DIFFERENT EXPERIENCES)

Now, when I serve as a member of search committees, I see that one of the ways candidates can set themselves apart is through a strong, focused written presentation. It may go without saying, but I am surprised at the number of candidates who submit cover letters and thick applications, but fail to tailor their qualifications and unique histories to our institution. Unbelievably, some candidates who use a mass production style forget to tailor their letter to our institution and leave in the name of another. The committee may see this as a source of great humor but, regrettably, it can be a deal breaker for even the most highly qualified candidate.

Today's accountability environment may make hiring White applicants in predominantly White colleges a high stakes activity. Individuals who have not traditionally seen themselves as having a race (e.g., White applicants) will find that they must consider the ways their membership in the racial power hierarchy impacts the culture of higher education. I would advise all candidates to be very well prepared to answer thoughtfully and clearly the standard interview questions related to their understanding of multiculturalism or diversity. It has been my experience that candidates who tank on this question are considered to be out of the mainstream, isolated from changes in the global human experience, or adrift in a world that no longer exists. All things being equal, the candidate who misses this opportunity rarely advances to the next level of selection.

I would also recommend that the candidate consider what other questions might be raised in any general meeting or open "meet the candidate" venue. For example, when our campus was searching for a provost I attended open faculty sessions to hear responses to my favorite question. I asked each applicant "Will you identify, please, a book that you have read in that last year? Will you talk a little bit about how that book relates to ideas associated with becoming a generally educated person?" Our campus was in the midst of an overhaul of our general education program and I was assuming the candidates familiarized themselves with our general education program and read for their own growth and development. Imagine the negative impact when candidates couldn't identify any book at all, or selected something related to trends in higher education and made the faculty collectively cringe. Or, better, imagine our insight when one applicant said he hadn't read much lately and then after a long silence named Machiavellli's *The Prince* as his book. The general education lesson? How to lead. It was a startling response. We eventually hired a different applicant for the position. Her qualifications were outstanding. But equally powerful was her spontaneous demonstration on how to use a question to say something compelling about texts and learning, something at the very heart of the faculty experience.

Jill M. Schultz, PhD
Professor, Social Science Department
Frederick Community College

CHAPTER 11

The On-campus Interview in the Academic Search Process: A Retrospective View

By Frank Main

After nineteen years as a division chair, having conducted or supervised more than twenty-five search committees, I have experienced success and failure in the process. In the pages that follow I will offer a brief narrative about three critical elements in the search process. When candidates and academic units are successful, the counselor education program and the candidate connect on all three of these issues and an exciting journey begins.

THREE EFFECTIVE STRATEGIES FOR THE ACADEMIC SEARCH PROCESS

I have always encouraged search processes that allow candidates to engage their would-be colleagues both professionally and personally. The smaller the academic unit, the more important the interpersonal dispositions become in the test of "goodness of fit." "Fit" is the academic unit's code for the candidate's capacity to be accepted and join with the personalities and academic preparation of the unit's faculty members. The academic unit wants to know the candidate's preparation for and willingness to teach the courses that must be taught.

With respect to interpersonal dispositions, successful candidates do not have to acquiesce to all the personalities at the table, but they must show their capacity to recognize and respond appropriately to everyone. With respect to goodness of academic fit, if the unit has invited a candidate to campus, it has done so based on the materials the candidate has submitted. Therefore, the search process ought to include structured opportunities for the candidate to self-select topics and courses in the unit's curriculum and to identify any of his or her unique skills that are well anchored in the job announcement. Programs take great care in preparing the advertisement to ensure success; candidates need to pay close attention to it.

THREE ATTRIBUTES OF A SUCCESSFUL SEARCH

Candidates must exhibit keen interest in their prospective colleagues, the work that will define them, and their potential sense of place in the academic unit. Successful candidates overtly and thoroughly demonstrate their dispositions in each of these areas. I will address each of these dispositions briefly.

Candidates show interest in prospective colleagues

Successful candidates express keen interest in prospective colleagues—they do their homework. Today, this task is easily accomplished through brief web searches for the scholarly and academic interests of the unit's faculty. Publications and grant activities highlight each faculty member's passion and expertise. A review of current publications will illustrate how and with whom a faculty member works. This is important to both junior and senior applicants. As a candidate, it is helpful to learn how collegial the faculty is, and this is often expressed in co-authorships and partnerships. If a candidate has an opportunity, it can be helpful to ask, "How do you hope the person you hire will contribute to the work you're doing?"

Candidates can express curiosity about ongoing research and, in the process, communicate appreciation and respect for the work of their prospective colleagues. They are also able to communicate forethought and awareness of departmental scholarship and interpersonal chemistry. The point of this curiosity is not to engage in competitive banter but to show and express professional appreciation. All of these gestures help to establish a sense of fit for the program and a sense of belonging for the applicant. Of course these curiosities must be reflected in their preparation.

Candidates recognize what the department needs

Successful candidates express a passion for the work that needs to be done as well as the work they might like to do. Candidates seeking careers in academia, while perhaps inspired by the academic life, must be aware of current, practical departmental needs. A quick review of web-based class schedules can provide an estimate of the department's unmet needs: the candidate can identify courses taught by "staff," graduate students, or adjunct faculty not listed as regular program faculty. Astute candidates see what needs to be done, note courses they are qualified to teach, and volunteer to do so. Less curious candidates often respond to questions about what they can and would like to teach by offering a wish list of courses that may not currently be offered by the program. This is not to say that an applicant's vision is not of value to the unit, but candidates must grasp the difference between their own ambitions and the existing unit culture and institutional strategic priorities. Again, this information is usually available in the public domain of the university and can be found by searching the university's web pages.

Candidates recognize their need for a sense of place

Finally, successful candidates seek opportunities during the interview process to identify their sense of place within the program and community. Candidates must attend to both, but ought to prioritize them: First, they must be able to see their opportunities for a professional sense of place. Second, they must be able to be comfortable with their fit in the region, locale, and culture.

Professionally, candidates must examine how well the work required fits their work ethics and professional goals. For example, how does the institution prioritize the virtues of teaching and research? This value can usually be estimated in a couple of ways. First, how have the institution's programs been classified by the Carnegie Foundation for The Advancement of Teaching (http://www.carnegiefoundation.org/classifications/)? While there is not a straight line between an institution's classification and prioritization of teaching and research, enough information is provided here to infer how teaching and research will be generally weighted during the tenure and promotion process. The most basic distinction, of course, is whether the institution offers both the doctoral and entry-level degree or the entry-level degree alone. Although there are eighteen Carnegie graduate classifications, doctoral versus post-baccalaureate degrees are the major distinguishing index. Candidates can quickly look up their institutions of interest to estimate workloads and research expectations, and they should go to the interview with full knowledge of these expectations.

The details of these expectations can be further defined during the interview process by asking specific questions about tenure and promotion. The information thus obtained can be reconciled with the publication records of the unit's tenured faculty members. Finally, counselor education programs have unique identities that are passed on by word-of-mouth or reputation, and this information is easily accessible through formal and informal sources. Most notable, of course, is whether the institution's advertisement required or preferred that applicants be graduates of CACREP accredited institutions.

All of this information should provide candidates with a robust sense of how their work will be defined and valued at a particular institution. Candidates must ask themselves and their advisors if they are prepared to direct dissertations and if they want their work and academic careers to be weighted and evaluated accordingly. In the final analysis, the only relevant criterion by which to assess a successful search is whether or not the person who gets the job keeps it!

Candidates who become associate professors know who they are, professionally; they base their career searches and decisions on an earnest personal assessment. They know the answers to these questions: "Am I defined by my joy of teaching and my relationships with students, or am I defined by my scholarship? And do I recognize my propensities when I am out of balance?" These questions are not meant to be dichotomous—they simply bring into focus the dialectical interaction between scholarship and pedagogy, and clarify our position on the continuum of autonomy and belonging. Each of us is aware of our tendency to become disoriented or imbalanced at times, and we are also well aware of our propensity to lean in one direction or the other. In the final analysis, this is the most relevant determinant of whether a candidate becomes an associate professor or not. Based upon institution values, teaching and research are usually weighted one over the other. Candidates must know or be capable of estimating how their predilections and gifts will fit the institutional culture.

The last priority, with respect to sense of place, is literal. How do the region, locale, and culture fit the candidate's identity, and what are the limits of the candidate's capacity to bloom and grow where he or she is planted? While we are all committed to change, our capacity to put down roots may be limited by surprising and deceptively simple things—e.g., "I'm surprised by how much I miss the water!" Successful candidates proactively consider whether the place will physically provide a nurturing climate. How will the community offer a sense of place with respect to work, friends, family, and spirituality? Each of these indices must be apparent to the candidate, or investment in the process will be for naught.

In summary, a career in counselor education is far more than a job; a career in counselor education is a calling and a passion. Although most counselor educators serve at two or three institutions during the course of their careers, not many leave the profession. Upon finding the right fit, their tenure is generally measured in decades.

CONCLUSIONS

Candidates and programs are obligated to formally address each of these issues in the interview process. The candidate and the program must have a structured opportunity to express their respective desires for personal and programmatic development, and candidates should be given an opportunity to give voice to their passions, as should current unit faculty members.

Ideally, candidates are also given the opportunity to express their perceived sense of professional belonging. They must be able to see that they will be able to meet the expectations of an associate professor with integrity. Indeed, programs must be prepared to make the tenure and promotion process as transparent as possible.

Finally, the candidate and program should be forthright about the capacity of the place to provide a nurturing sense of belonging. The ultimate measure of success in the academic search process culminates in the promotion of a junior faculty member to associate professor; when it happens, it is anchored in mutual commitment.

Frank Main, EdD
Retired, Professor
University of South Dakota

CHAPTER 12

The Academic Job Search as an Exciting Time: Taking Pragmatic Steps to Land a Position in Higher Education

By Jim Saiers

I decided to attend graduate school after reading an article published in a 1988 issue of *Newsweek*. The article identified environmental consulting as a fast-growing field in which I could make a comfortable living, provided that I earned a master's degree in environmental sciences. Soon after I entered graduate school, I discovered that I really enjoyed research, so I traded in my aspirations of a career in environmental consulting and hunkered down for a PhD. I hoped to land a university position where I could conduct research, mentor students, and teach. Since 1995, the year I finished my dissertation, I have applied for more than a dozen faculty positions, received more rejection letters than I care to remember, interviewed at six universities, been offered five jobs, and accepted two. In the following paragraphs, I offer some advice that draws on my job-hunting experience and on my experiences from the other side of the desk, when I have interviewed faculty candidates.

Preparation for a faculty position starts long before you begin preparing your curriculum vitae and cover letter. An applicant's potential to succeed as a faculty member at a research-oriented university is measured largely in terms of scholarship, which, for natural scientists of all varieties, is demonstrated through publication in peer-reviewed journals. Don't wait until your dissertation is bound or until your postdoctoral appointment is complete to begin submitting papers that document your research findings. Instead, you should publish as you go. I am not suggesting that you thin-slice your research, as one good paper in a top-notch journal is worth more than twice as many mediocre papers. You should, however, write up each substantive component of your research as soon as the data are collected, analyzed, and interpreted. Writing is hard work—harder than anything else we do—and your success in the academic job market requires that you do it well and in a timely way.

You can further improve your competitiveness in the job market by getting involved in the scientific community. Become a member of your field's major scientific society and attend its conferences. At these conferences, you will get a glimpse of recent research discoveries before they appear in press, and, equally important, you will have an opportunity to make a positive impression on other members of your field by presenting your own research results. There is much more to these conferences than science; they are also social events. You will meet graduate students from other universities who may one day become your friends, your collaborators, or the reviewers of your grant proposals, and you will have the opportunity to interact with senior faculty, who may soon be reviewing your job application.

About a year before your anticipated graduation, you should shift some of your attention away from your scholarly activities and toward the job-application process. An application packet for a university faculty position consists of a curriculum vitae, a cover letter that outlines your research and teaching interests, and the names of three to five people who can write you a recommendation if you make the "short list" of applicants. The content of the curriculum vitae is rather standard (although the format is not) and should include information on college and graduate education, professional experience, honors and recognition, publications, conference presentations, research grants, courses taught, professional affiliations, and service to your school and scientific community. Although the curriculum vitae will not change much from application to application, the cover letter should.

The purpose of the cover letter is to convince the members of the search committee that your research and teaching will substantially strengthen their program. You should include a description of your current research, discuss its implications, and make a case for its relevance. Keep in mind your audience. Most of the search committee will not share your expertise, so you should avoid jargon and excessive detail. Explain what you are doing and why it's important, but don't go overboard on the description of *how* you are doing your research unless your methodologies are truly groundbreaking. Once you have outlined your current research, you should demonstrate that you are looking beyond graduate school and have a plan for succeeding as a junior-faculty member. In a paragraph or two, describe some ways in which you could extend your current research and identify new lines of research that you'd pursue if hired. Tailor your letter by explaining how your research plans complement the department's existing pool of expertise, fill a gap in current coverage, or could lead to collaborations with particular members of the faculty.

Your cover letter should include a statement on teaching, too. If you are just finishing your graduate degree or postdoctoral appointment, you may have had little opportunity to teach. This won't necessarily be perceived as a weakness, especially if you are a natural scientist or engineer applying for a position at a research-oriented university. Avoid trying to craft a statement on teaching philosophy if you have not taught. Chances are you don't have one, and you will not be able to convince an experienced teacher that you do. Instead, identify two or three courses and briefly describe the content and objectives for each one. Your choice of courses should be informed, at least in part, by the hiring department's needs. This information may be revealed in the job advertisement or through a telephone conversation with the search-committee chair. Alternatively, you may be able to identify curricular deficiencies by examining the courses listed on the department's website.

While it is important for your proposed courses to fill a niche, there are additional criteria that should guide your course selection. In particular, you should identify courses that you would enjoy developing and be enthusiastic about teaching. Failure to attend to these two criteria will lead to misery for you (and your students).

The importance of what you say in your cover letter may be exceeded only by what others say about you. Your letters of recommendation will be scrutinized and weighed heavily by the search committee, so you must choose your letter-writers with exceptional care. You need letters of *strong* recommendation supported by knowledge of your academic preparation, research contributions, and interpersonal skills. Most recommendation letters are positive and many are full of superlatives, but only those that substantiate their claims through specific examples of an applicant's abilities will lead to an on-campus interview. These letters require considerable effort to compose, so don't assume that everyone will do it. An individual's willingness to write a recommendation for you is not enough. When you approach a potential reference, don't just ask "Could you write me a letter of recommendation?" Rather, probe further and ask "Do you have an adequate knowledge of my academic background and a sufficiently favorable impression of my accomplishments to write a letter of strong recommendation?" You are likely to get an honest response that could disappoint you at first, but will ultimately result in a stronger application.

Once you submit your application, there are two possible outcomes. One of these is bad. The odds are that you (and many others) will eventually receive a politely worded rejection letter from the search-committee chair. This letter will almost certainly be devoid of useful information. It will not explain what led to the rejection. Maybe your expertise wasn't right, or your publication record wasn't strong enough, or perhaps the search committee wanted someone with postdoctoral experience and you are a freshly minted PhD. You may never know the reason, so there is no use dwelling on the rejection. Polish your vitae, edit your cover letter, and submit your improved application in response to the next job opening. It only costs the price of a stamp.

Eventually your perseverance will pay off, and the search-committee chair will invite you for an interview. At this point, your odds of landing the job have substantially increased, because only three to five candidates are invited for an on-campus interview. The on-campus visits are usually two-day affairs in which you meet with members of the search committee, other faculty, students, and administrators. The interviews may be conducted by groups of faculty, but usually you will be scheduled for a series of one-on-one interviews, each lasting thirty to forty-five minutes. Consider requesting the interview itinerary from the search-committee chair so you can learn about the professional background of the people you will be meeting. The conversations with your hosts will be more enjoyable and productive if you are able to talk intelligently about *their* research and teaching interests.

Most of the interview will be about you, however. Be prepared to answer questions about your preparation for the position, what courses you can teach, and the direction of your future research. You will also be asked, probably several times, why you are interested in a position within their department. Your response should demonstrate your knowledge of the university, department, and its faculty. Faculty often end the meeting by asking the candidate for questions. This is your chance to interview them and to gather information to help you decide if a position within their department is right for you. Steer clear of questions about salary and other conditions of a potential offer, but do inquire about factors that will influence your working environment: teaching load, expectations for tenure, and student quality.

You are likely to be so immersed in the interviews that you will have no time to get nervous about presenting your research seminar. Typically, one hour is allotted for the seminar, but you should limit your presentation to forty-five minutes. Any longer and you will lose the attention of your audience and will not have time for questions. The quality and impact of your research will be judged largely on the basis of the seminar, so fine-tune the content and practice your delivery.

Preparation for a research seminar is challenging because your audience will be diverse in their scientific training, and few people, if any, will be experts in your sub-specialty. Therefore, it is incumbent upon you to explain the practical, scientific, and societal issues that motivate your work. You also should summarize, at least in a conceptual way, theory that is requisite to the interpretation of your results. Finally, you should discuss the significance and implications of your conclusions. It is important to convey the rigor of your work, but avoid long explanations of complex technical issues, as these will be distracting (or boring) and jeopardize the audience's understanding of what is most important.

You will be worn out by the end of the interview and be relieved as you board the plane home. Now the waiting begins. You may learn quickly —within a day or two—or you may have to wait for weeks as other candidates are interviewed. If the good news of an offer does come, you will probably receive it in a telephone call from the chair of the search committee or head of the department. You should be excited, and it is appropriate to express your pleasure, but play it close to the vest, as the negotiation process is about to begin.

There are many components of an offer package, in addition to your annual salary, and most are open for negotiation. Startup funds to support the purchase of laboratory, field, and computer equipment often receive the greatest attention. Depending on the discipline and the institution, startup funds for junior faculty range from tens of thousands of dollars to hundreds of thousands of dollars. The department head will probably ask what you need for startup. Develop a list of equipment and supplies necessary for you to launch a successful research program, and request an amount that covers their costs. Other components of an offer package open for negotiation include: summer salary, usually for the first two years of an appointment; an initial reduction in teaching load that allows extra time for grant-proposal writing and laboratory setup; funds for graduate student stipend and tuition; and the amount of laboratory space. You will find that the university is flexible in some areas, but unwilling to give an inch (or extra dollar) in others. If you are able to negotiate an offer package that is acceptable to you, make sure you get all the conditions in writing with the appropriate signatures. This document may not be legally binding, but a written record provides increased assurance that the terms of your agreement will be honored.

As you become immersed in the negotiation process, you may forget, at least temporarily, that there is more to life than work. You (and your spouse) have to be content living in the community in which you work. Before you accept any offer, you should revisit the campus and surrounding area to identify potential places to live, estimate commuting times, collect information on schools (if you have children), and learn about recreational opportunities. The university will probably be willing to pay for this second visit and may even arrange for a real-estate agent or someone else with local knowledge to show you around the area. This is an exciting time. Be sure you enjoy it!

Jim Saiers, PhD
Professor, Hydrology, School of Environmental Studies
Yale University

CHAPTER 13

Finding the Right Faculty Position: The Importance of Fit

By James Machell

Having a lot of experience in the job-search process may be akin to being expert at creating manuscripts that are never accepted for publication. Both are ego-involved processes that can lead to frustration and anxiety, yet both can be excellent learning opportunities if approached appropriately. While having a manuscript accepted for publication always seems like a good outcome, the same may not hold true for being offered and accepting positions in higher learning institutions.

In what follows, I outline what I believe to be the importance of fit, or good match, between one seeking a position and the organization where employment is sought. The first section provides an overview of the importance of understanding one's interests, knowledge, skills, competencies, and dispositions, and how they compare with the vision, mission, goals, expectations, and reward systems of different types of colleges of universities. The second section addresses some of the political realities that need to be considered when undertaking the job search. The value of the learning that can occur in the search process is briefly addressed in the third section. The final section addresses practicalities based on personal experiences on both ends of the endeavor, in seeking positions and in making hiring decisions.

THE IMPORTANCE OF FIT

New doctoral-degree holders often have considerable debt, and there is a real temptation to apply for every job available in your discipline. While landing a job, beginning an academic career, and realizing a real paycheck are not to be minimized, my advice is to be selective in the search process. The approach I advocate is to conduct a self-assessment as a first step to identify your individual interests, knowledge, skills, and competencies. Novice faculty-members emerge from doctoral programs with varying amounts of aptitude, experience, and interest related to teaching, research, and other areas of responsibility. It is important to know in which areas your talents, interests, and desire for accomplishment are most focused.

Once you have completed a self-assessment, the next step is to identify institutions searching for faculty that are a good fit. The *Higher Education Directory*, published by Higher Education Publications, Inc., is a valuable reference tool; it can help you to quickly gather information pertaining to Carnegie Classification, enrollment, and other pertinent data. It is likely that someone at your doctoral institution has a copy.

While all faculty positions involve activities related to teaching, scholarship, and service, the degree of emphasis placed on each area varies by institution. These three primary areas of responsibility are not unrelated, but in determining your fit with an organization, it is important to know the proportion in they are valued and rewarded.

Colleges and universities vary across multiple dimensions, including mission, vision, geographic location, size, and others. Expectations for faculty members vary as well, according to the same dimensions. Normally, for you to be successful at a doctorate-granting research institution will require the ability to fulfill an ambitious research agenda that culminates in publications in upper-echelon journals and success obtaining extramural funding through grants. Universities with roots as "normal" schools—master's colleges and universities, baccalaureate colleges, regional state universities, and community colleges—as a rule, place a greater emphasis on faculty members' success as teachers and ability to provide good service to various constituents within and without the academic community.

Faculty workloads vary according to institutional type, mission, and goals. A typical teaching load for a new faculty member at an institution with a research focus is six to nine hours per semester. At such institutions, new faculty members are often provided with additional time during the first semester or first academic year to get their research agendas under way. At schools where a greater emphasis is placed on teaching, faculty typically teach between twelve and fifteen hours per semester in undergraduate programs, and between nine and twelve hours per semester at the graduate level.

Much can be learned by searching college and university websites. I would suggest finding the administration section of the site first, and reviewing the history, mission, vision, strategic plan, and other guiding documents for the institution. The "academic affairs" section is also valuable in terms of finding guiding documents. Some institutions have articulated an educational-philosophy statement, or similar document, that is telling in terms of what is expected of faculty and students in the teaching/learning interchange. It is also important to learn as much as possible about the college and department in which your prospective position is located.

Anxiety related to tenure and promotion among higher-education faculty is quite common. For this reason, I would strongly encourage you to find the policies and practices associated with reviewing faculty for tenure and promotion. In many institutions, these will be contained in a faculty handbook or something similar. These documents should reveal information associated with the number of years of service required to become eligible for review for tenure and promotion, and criteria used in making recommendations. Being able to see these performance targets is useful in determining the degree of fit between the individual and the institution.

Having determined the type of institution that appears to be a good fit, it is then a matter of finding posted faculty positions, such as those found in the *Chronicle of Higher Education* or on other websites like HigherEdJobs.com. The first step in this process is identifying positions in your discipline at all institutions that meet your criteria for fit. Then, I would encourage prioritizing of this list by other factors. These could include cost of living, proximity to areas of personal interest, and quality-of-life indicators.

Once you have completed these steps, you will begin preparing and submitting applications. Other chapters in this work address practical aspects of preparing letters of application, vitae, references, and other materials you will submit. Advice on preparing for and engaging in interviews and campus visits is also provided elsewhere in the text. In what follows, I offer some ideas related to some of the politics associated with faculty searches.

POLITICS, TIMING, AND INSIDE CANDIDATES

Hiring faculty members and administrators is the most important and costly decision colleges and universities make. Without good faculty members and leadership, an institution of higher learning has little chance of being successful. Given the importance of the process, politics are sure to be involved.

One layer of politics has to do with bias. We all have biases; the best we can do is articulate them and recognize them as we make decisions.

The biases of those serving on faculty screening committees may manifest, for example, as inclinations toward or against applicants who have graduated from certain higher-learning institutions. Other biases that may factor into how your application and candidacy are viewed have to do with past experiences in teaching, service, and research, or whether your institutional affiliations have been with public or private institutions of higher learning. Some may have a bias toward those with strong interpersonal skills or dispositions related to being more interested in the collective good rather than an individual focus. It is not possible to know all of the biases that come into play in the search and screening process; you must simply accept this as part of seeking employment.

Another layer of politics that is often obscure has to do with inside candidates. In searching for faculty positions, it is possible that there are other candidates in the pool of applicants who have gained traction with the unit through previous associations in professional organizations, collaborative research activities, or teaching within the unit on a part-time or adjunct basis. People tend to be less fearful about known commodities, so inside candidates are often seen as preferable to other candidates about whom less is known through direct experience.

Timing is another factor that is mysterious in the search and selection process. Great variance exists in the amount of time it will take to receive communication about each step in the process. Normally, guidelines and deadlines for submitting application materials are made clear. The amount of time it might take to receive communication about whether you are still being considered may range from a few days to several months. Based on my experience, I would encourage you never to assume that you have been eliminated from consideration until you receive communication. Universities are known to move at glacial speed, and this may be truer in search processes than in many other decision-making events.

THE VALUE OF LEARNING FROM THE EXPERIENCE

It is natural to experience disappointment when not selected. Yet these can be and should be excellent learning events if we are, as most people expect of educational professionals, life-long learners. At each step of the process, one should reflect and share with a mentor or friend what occurred, what seemed to work well, and how you might refine your approach. This is true for everything from writing a letter of application to the format of your vitae, from your preparation for interviewing to the questions you have prepared to ask of those with whom you interview. For me, the experience of being a finalist for two dean positions prior to being selected was of great value, despite the frustration of learning later that inside candidates were selected in both of the cases when I was not. It should be added here that following events associated with one of these dean searches on the university website (which was a very transparent process in many respects) helped me to realize early on that there was an inside candidate. Again, there is much to be learned from going through a campus visit and interview process.

PRACTICALITIES

The practical suggestions offered here are based on my personal experiences as a candidate for faculty and dean positions and as a faculty member and dean on the hiring end of the exchange. My first piece of advice is to do your homework. By this I mean to learn everything you can about an institution to which you apply. If you have followed the earlier advice offered about determining the fit between what you have to offer and the institution, it becomes much easier to explain how you can help the organization accomplish its mission and goals. You should be able to determine recent accomplishments and new initiatives in the university, college, and department in which you are interested. You should also be able to determine institutional policies and expectations regarding faculty members. This information will serve you well during telephone or face-to-face interviews. Nothing makes a worse impression on committee members than your not demonstrating knowledge about the institution. It is a sign of disrespect.

Your letter of application needs to be specific. If you have been thorough in your self-assessment and determination of fit, your letter should speak clearly to your interests and your ability to help the department and college advance their agenda and goals. Savvy committee members have a keen eye for generic letters. If you take the approach of copy-and-pasting, be careful to proofread. I have seen letters indicating interest in the position that, unfortunately, identified another institution.

In creating your list of references, it is helpful to include some references from outside your doctoral-granting institution. Be sure to include references that have knowledge of your abilities as a teacher, scholar, and service-provider, since these are the primary areas of responsibility. Even though it is not stated, it will also be helpful if your references can speak to such basic traits as initiative, trustworthiness, interpersonal abilities, and ability to work well as a part of a team.

Additional artifacts, such as teaching evaluations (if you have had the opportunity to teach at the college level) and those related to your scholarship, such as off-prints of publications or manuscripts you have submitted, can be very helpful. In my experiences on search committees and as a dean reviewing committees' recommendations, I always find this type of information to be a rich source of additional evidence that is influential in determining a candidate's potential for contributing to the academic community.

In terms of interviewing, several points are important. You should rehearse responding to likely questions. Asking a mentor or peer to conduct a mock interview is especially helpful. Always be prepared for questions related to how you will work with students and colleagues, and to your teaching philosophy. Even if your research agenda is not fully developed, be ready to relate your areas of research interest and one or more studies you have in mind. Naturally, it is important to be honest, even if what you have to say is not what you think the committee wants to hear. This is also a sign of a possible bad fit. It is not fatal to say "I don't know," so long as you don't have to rely on this response too often. Even though you are likely to be nervous during campus visits and on-site interviews, it is helpful to be as relaxed, warm, and open as possible without being overly friendly.

Finally, I encourage taking some time to reflect on your experiences once you have completed a campus visit and/or interview. Being asked illegal questions, sensing an environment that makes you uncomfortable, observing negative body language from individuals on the committee, and other similar negative aspects of a visit or interview should serve as warning signs that this might not be the right place for you. The people included in the visit's schedule can also be telling. Did you meet with the dean and/or one of the vice presidents for academic affairs? Were students a part of the process? All of these aspects of campus visits and interviews are sources of information for you to consider.

TWO FINAL THOUGHTS

You may not have the luxury of being able to follow this advice, but I have learned that the best time to find a job is when you do not need a job. By this, I mean that it is much less stressful and makes more sense to search for positions when you already have a position that is at least somewhat satisfying and rewarding. It is easy to take a position, experience success, and become comfortable. Sometimes junior faculty-members find themselves in such an enviable position but, for one reason or another, see the need to seek a change. Perhaps you wish to get closer, geographically, to aging parents, or to other family or friends. Sometimes a person simply feels the need for a new challenge, an important aspect of career progression.

A side benefit to exploring opportunities while satisfactorily employed is the leverage a job offer from another institution can provide. At some institutions, the only way to enjoy a salary increase not associated with promotion in rank is to begin negotiations with a job offer in hand. Personally, I find this distasteful and a terrible waste of resources (that is, using other institutions' searches for your personal benefit, fully aware that you do not want a different position), but that is a current reality at some universities.

One of the great ironies of the tenure and promotion process in higher education is that once you have invested several years, performed well, and received tenure and/or advanced rank at one institution, it becomes more difficult to leave. You will note that most faculty positions advertised are at the rank of assistant professor. To consider moving after several years of service and success in promotion and/or tenure candidacy requires being ready to negotiate for rank, knowing that it is possible to realize a reduction in rank and/or give up tenure by moving. More and more universities are moving to a larger percentage of non-tenure-track positions, making this prospect even more daunting.

I will close with the observation that the best opportunities come at the worst times. As much as we might like to create and execute a careful, detailed plan for our career and life, that is seldom the way things work. My experience has been that you must always be open to opportunities. It seems never to fail that when the time is right for a move, a position that would be a good fit is not available. Conversely, the best opportunities often arise at a time when leaving one position and moving to take another will create hardships. We are constantly juggling personal lives and professional duties. We must accept that to advance our careers often requires personal sacrifice. In the final analysis, you are in control of the decisions you make, and by having a good plan for finding the right fit, learning how to cope with political realities, and always looking at the process as an opportunity for learning, you will be successful.

James Machell, PhD
Dean, College of Education and Professional Studies
University of Central Oklahoma

CHAPTER 14

Interview Process and Candidate Selection for an Academic Position in Chemistry

By James D. Hoefelmeyer

Upon contemplating their career goals as chemists, many individuals find appeal in the academic setting. Positive aspects of academe include: the reward of crafting young minds in the classroom, creating a legacy through a lifetime of work in a field of study and through service missions, an element of self-determination in management of resources, and being in a unique position within the community as a source of knowledge. In this chapter, the application, interview, and selection process for the position of tenure-track assistant professor in chemistry will be discussed.

Upon beginning a job search, applicants should obtain a list of all job openings, then identify those that broadly match their qualifications, expectations, desires, and ambitions. Obviously, a match is truly identified when an applicant accepts an offer from a department; however, many questions remain unanswered until later stages in the application and interview process. For this reason, applicants should not be too restrictive when sending application packets, while at the same time not sending packets to departments that they have no intention of joining. Applicants should be ambitious, within reason, and not forgo sending an application to a department out of fear of rejection. This requires self-analysis, which can be difficult, but there are well-established metrics for identifying productive scientists, as well as those who possess leadership and teaching ability. These include publication record, presentations, proposals submitted/funded, number of contacts in the scientific community, teaching experience, students mentored, awards, and more. This sort of self-analysis is a composite assessment to which many individuals contribute. Applicants can use this picture to derive the closeness of match with faculty openings. Ultimately, the applicant's potential sphere of influence within the chemistry community should be consistent with that of the faculty in the department of interest.

Typically, the applicant will have obtained a PhD in chemistry, and completed some postdoctoral work. As a side note, the transition from PhD to postdoc is critical in the development of the young chemist. Moving to a new department, location, and project serves to broaden one's experience and test one's adaptability. Furthermore, in the postdoctoral position, one should take a leadership role in the activities in the lab. This may include taking responsibility for some details such as ordering, safety, organization of chemicals and supplies, orienting new group members with lab protocols, setting up a new lab or instrument, and participating in tasks like proposal-writing or substituting in lectures. In the postdoctoral role, one can demonstrate an ability to lead, interact, and communicate, all in addition to being an independent researcher. If one aspires to being a professor, it is worthwhile to let one's research advisor know. An advisor can share his or her own experience, and mentor young scientists in the academic role.

A central skill for a professor is the ability to communicate well. A faculty member will encounter several types of audience, such as students, faculty, administrators, program officers, scientists, politicians, business people, and the public. In addition, the importance of writing cannot be over-emphasized. The success of the academic chemist depends greatly on an ability to write proposals, manuscripts, evaluations, reviews, comments, letters, and learning texts. Therefore, it is strongly recommended that persons interested in an academic career take steps to become excellent writers, such as writing manuscripts and proposals, learning the writing conventions in the chemical literature, and taking a technical-writing course.

The assistant-professor position requires years of experience that are obtained during graduate and postdoctoral studies. During those years, the student will acquire experience as a scientist, communicator, and member of the local and university communities. Early in one's career, it may be difficult to realize how these experiences will eventually coalesce into a total profile that may fit a given academic position. Academic duties are tripartite, consisting of teaching, research, and service. As soon as a student realizes she wishes to become a professor, it is worthwhile to examine all of her activities in that context. She should take steps to perform in productive roles that contribute to career goals. This will help to develop a strong application packet, with lots of depth and plentiful evidence of her ability to flourish in academe.

The applicant should provide all of the materials requested for the posted position in the packet. An incomplete packet will result in lower probability of being selected by the search committee. Usually, an application packet contains a cover letter, vitae, description of proposed research, and statement of teaching philosophy. In addition, letters of recommendation (three to five) should arrive separately to support the application. A thoughtful cover letter directly addresses members of the chemistry department, and should briefly indicate why a potential match exists. A mention of some unique aspects of the department, such as instrument capabilities, research centers, or recent research thrusts shows the search committee that the applicant has taken time to think about the department.

The vitae is an information-rich document that provides a synopsis of the credentials and activities of an applicant, and is a foundation for the application packet. The information in the vitae should be formatted for rapid harvest by readers. A search committee needs to know about the educational background and professional preparation of the applicant. Professional activities, awards, presentations, publications, contact information, and references should be included. Headings such as Teaching Experience, Research Activities, and Research Interests can be useful as well.

In the statement of teaching philosophy, an applicant may describe an approach to teaching, motivation for teaching, and a list of courses of interest. Few people are naturally excellent teachers. Those few should provide clear evidence of teaching interest and success.

A description of proposed research constitutes the core of the application. It is important to provide exactly the material requested in the application solicitation. Some request research descriptions in shortened format, and others in more detailed format. Applicants should be able to describe their research projects in one-page abstract format, two to four page short descriptions, and five to ten page complete descriptions. Interestingly, many starter-type grants and pre-proposals only allow about two to four pages of text for the research description, while full proposals for such agencies as the National Science Foundation allow roughly eight pages. It is absolutely crucial that the writing is clear and the projects are thoughtful (i.e., soundly rooted in concepts in the literature, with a creative element of discovery and manageable risk).

Candidates' proposed projects should not be continuations of graduate or postdoctoral research. They should draw on candidates' experience and knowledge base. Candidates must be able to convince the committee that the projects are capable of garnering external funding, which requires the projects to be interesting and creative, to address significant problems in science, and to be well written.

Finally, letters of recommendation should be requested to support the application. These should be provided by individuals with detailed knowledge of the accomplishments and abilities of the applicant. A letter from the graduate advisor and postdoctoral advisor are a must, and additional letters may come from former thesis-committee members, teachers, or other individuals who are familiar with the research conducted by the applicant.

When requesting letters of recommendation, applicants should provide ample time to write the letter (two to four weeks), a CV and summary of achievements, a list of institutions to which to send the letter (with pre-addressed envelopes or electronic contact information), and the institutions' deadlines. All of this will expedite the process of writing the letter and ensure that it arrives with the application packet. It is important when requesting the letter to talk about the nature of the letter, and to have a mutual understanding that there is enthusiastic support for the applicant. Polite follow-ups help prevent late or forgotten letters.

With the application packet submitted, candidates wait as search committees begin the review process. The committee will only review applications after the deadline, and late applications are at a heavy disadvantage because they tend to complicate a review process already under way. Tens to hundreds of applications may be filed for an opening, and the search committee will sift through these and begin to eliminate deficient applications.

The vitae is the quickest way to learn about the applicants. It must be evident that they have the appropriate qualifications for the opening. The candidates' academic pedigrees will be an important consideration, and those who have worked with leading scientists will stand out. The search committee will look for candidates with profiles that ascend and strengthen over time. Applications can often be removed from further consideration after evaluation of the vitae alone. Reasons may include a background inconsistent with the job description, lack of experience or qualifications, or weak metrics as indicators of scientific productivity.

Applications that pass this initial inspection will receive further scrutiny. The evaluator will read the teaching philosophy, cover letter, research description, and letters of reference. The teaching philosophy and cover letter may reveal a candidate to be thoughtful, and can display writing ability and comprehension of the expectations associated with the position. Letters of reference are a key measure of the quality of the applicant. All of the letters should be supportive, and enthusiastic letters that richly detail the candidate's abilities and qualities provide a tremendous boost to the application. The research description will be examined for competency, creativity, its relation to current research programs in the department, and its likelihood of being funded. The search committee will review all of the applications, and produce a short-list of perhaps twenty-five candidates.

The short-list represents the current active candidate pool, and continually decreases until the committee makes an offer that is accepted. The next stage in the selection process may be to produce a refined short-list of roughly ten candidates to interview in a phone call.

When a candidate receives an invitation for a phone interview, she should move quickly to prepare. The invitation may lead the phone interview by only a few days. During this time, the candidate can investigate the department, its faculty, and the university in detail. This information will be valuable during the phone conversation, and can provide entry points to discussion. The candidate may write out anticipated questions and formulate thoughtful responses. This is also a good time to produce a list of questions to ask the committee. During the phone interview, it is helpful to speak from a location without distractions, to be alert, and to have information at the ready.

Successful interviews often flow more like a conversation, with a two-way exchange of information, than a series of questions and answers. When given an opportunity to speak, the candidate should answer questions clearly, while making a few key points. Short and predictable responses leave room for uncomfortable silences. A thoughtful answer that engages the search committee will make a positive impression, often spurring additional discussion. The applicant's ability to interact with the faculty can be revealed here. Candidates should attempt to avoid coming across as inexperienced or uninformed with respect to the tripartite academic mission. After completing the phone interviews, the search committee will deliberate and select perhaps three candidates for on-site interviews. During the phone interview, a candidate may inquire about the timeline for the selection process.

On-site interviews may follow phone interviews on the order of a few weeks. The interview may span one or two full days on campus. The nature of the interview will vary for each institution, and will involve meeting with several of the faculty in the chemistry department; with administrators, such as the dean or head of the Office of Research; and with the chair of the department. Candidates will present a seminar based on data obtained during graduate/postdoctoral research. Most departments will request a presentation of proposed research, and some departments may request a teaching lecture. As with the phone interview, the candidate should take the time to learn about the research of the faculty, collaborative efforts in the department, recent activities (e.g., infrastructure-development or major grants), student curriculum, and institution profile.

The interview schedule is jam-packed with activities, from early breakfast to dinner, and leaves little time for personal reflection. It is important to be adaptable, conversational, resilient, polite, and attentive, all while radiating an air of control, calm, and thoughtfulness. The day may start with breakfast with one or two faculty members. The candidate should greet the faculty with a smile, and let them know she's pleased to visit. She should engage in friendly conversation over breakfast, and try to learn something about those in her company.

After breakfast, the candidate will probably meet with faculty members throughout the morning. Each meeting may last thirty to forty-five minutes. In these one-on-one visits, the faculty member will develop an impression of the candidate. Often, the faculty member will start off with friendly chatter, then move toward an introduction of his or her current research. This is a neat way to learn about the research programs of other chemists in a sort of speed-dating format. The candidate should express interest in the topic, and develop a two-way discussion about the research. This means being knowledgeable, attentive, and inquisitive. Being confrontational or testy and interrupting too often do not make positive impressions.

Lunch will arrive more quickly than anticipated. A few members of the department will join the candidate. Some of the lunch party may be faculty members with whom the candidate has already met. These friendly faces can serve as nucleation points for conversation, since the candidate may be gaining some sense of their speaking styles, ideas, and demeanors. This can be helpful for the candidate in getting to know the unfamiliar people at the table. Avoid being a stuffed shirt: be friendly, and have interesting things to say. Enjoy lunch—consume the nutrients necessary to carry you through the day, and avoid heavy foods that will cause the digestive tract to rumble later on. There are several more meetings with faculty members and administrators to go.

There may be a short break before the research seminar, which is typically at 4 p.m. But since visits may fall behind schedule, there might not be much time for a break, and what time there is will be needed to set up hardware in the lecture hall for the seminar. Lecture slides should be saved on a portable memory device, such as USB drive, as well as on a laptop computer. It is best to use one's own computer for the presentation, so as to avoid embarrassing technical snafus. One of the faculty will assist in setting up for the presentation. The candidate should make full use of this person's presence to set up, get water and a pointer, and chat while seats are filling up.

Soon after, the candidate will be introduced and deliver a smashing research seminar. Knowledge and confidence are key, here. The presentation should last forty-five minutes to allow time for questions. It is a mistake to speak for too long, and it is to the candidate's advantage to address questions from the audience. (Also of note: this day-long interview schedule resembles that of a guest seminar-speaker, which is a regular occurrence in the academic world.)

Other components of the on-site interview may vary by institution, and could include a teaching lecture and/or presentation of proposed research. The teaching lecture can be quite challenging, since candidates may not have extensive experience in the classroom. The closest approximation to teaching in a classroom might be group-meeting presentations. Group meetings require detailed presentations (slideshow or chalkboard format), and are typically interrupted with questions and discussion. The search committee should indicate the course and topic for the teaching lecture. In preparation for the lecture, make a set of notes to follow. This will help to structure and organize the lecture. Important components of the lecture include clear oration and diction, developing good eye contact with the audience, clear and organized board-work, and thoughtful content. I recommend using a chalkboard versus slideshows. Be flexible with notes and time management to avoid running beyond the class period.

Not all institutions will request a teaching lecture, preferring to focus on the candidate's description of proposed research. The environment for this presentation is somewhat less formal (perhaps over lunch), with an audience of faculty members only. Again, previous group-meeting presentations are a source of experience for this interview component. In a thirty to forty-five minute talk, the candidate will describe the significance of the proposed research, plan of action, and projected budget, lab space, and personnel needs. The discussion of the budget should include plans to obtain external funds. The proposed research should include one or two big-vision projects, with an outline of how those projects can branch out into tasks for undergraduate students, postdocs, and graduate students. The projects should be self-propelled or inexhaustible, meaning that results and data provide insights that lead to future projects. During the presentation, the candidate should project excitement about the proposed research that generates interest among the faculty.

The on-site interview is a two-way exchange of information, and the candidate should take the opportunity to learn as much about the institution as possible. Critical information may include the instrumentation in the department (and campus), the lab space immediately available, estimated startup funds, teaching loads, the promotion and tenure process, and the climate of the department (and campus). A great way to learn about these is to ask for a tour. The candidate may ask about the access, scheduling, and fee structure for instrumentation, as well as plans for new acquisitions. The candidate will assess whether the chemistry department has the infrastructure and facilities necessary to build a research program. Departments compete for good candidates just as candidates compete for positions. During the visit, the candidate should make sure that his or her questions are answered, and clearly express his or her own needs and vision as part of launching a new academic career.

The interview may conclude with a formal dinner with some of the faculty. The candidate may be feeling some relief that the intense schedule is winding down. The candidate should enjoy a delicious meal and let the faculty treat him or her to a relaxing experience. A candidate that expresses controlled enthusiasm about the day's events, recalling specific points, may impact the faculty positively. Be polite, smiling, and positive during the dinner, and avoid projecting a feeling of exhaustion. Over-consumption to the point of being sloppy or delaying the dinner should be avoided. At the conclusion of dinner, the candidate should thank the faculty for their company and the opportunity to visit.

A successful candidate will receive an informal offer from the department chair. The candidate should review the offer (for no more than two weeks, typically), and specifically request items to be included in the final written offer. Points to negotiate include salary, time frame for tenure-review, lab space, startup funds, students/postdocs included in startup, etc. All of the important points should be included in the written final offer. The candidate should avoid delays in communicating with the department.

Many resources exist to assist chemists searching for academic positions. The American Chemical Society website (ACS Careers) contains information about salaries and professional advancement, advice, and a job-search tool. Job openings appear in several publications, such as *Chemical and Engineering News*, the *Chronicle of Higher Education*, or *Science*. Colleagues, advisors, and friends can be especially useful for advice, proofreading, mock interviews, etc. Many campuses (and chemistry departments) have job-placement staff that can assist in the search process. Throughout the search, the candidate's inner motivations, passion for discovery and science, and determination will likely lead to a successful match with a fresh tenure-track faculty position.

James D. Hoefelmeyer, PhD
Assistant Professor, Chemistry
The University of South Dakota

CHAPTER 15

From Professional to Professor: Reflections on Mid-career Entry into Higher Education

By Phillip F. Diller

After twenty-four years as a public school teacher and administrator, I seized an opportunity to apply for a crossover position in higher education. The new tenure-track position for which I was ultimately hired involved directing the work of the university laboratory school and teaching undergraduate and graduate courses in education. The application and selection process appeared to be similar to the familiar process in public education: a paper application, a meeting with a screening committee that included faculty and administrators, a demonstration of teaching, a second interview with administration, and, finally, an interview with the institution's top-ranking administrators. The process paralleled selection and hiring processes I had experienced in five different school districts in several different states. However, the strong involvement of faculty in the process foreshadowed the organizational differences between basic and higher education, differences that were to impress and occasionally befuddle me for the next several years.

Generally speaking, public school districts are hierarchical organizations. Principals are in charge of teachers, teachers are in charge of students, and a superintendent oversees them all. From the outside, higher education appears similar: students report to professors, professors to deans, and deans to provosts and presidents. But it soon became apparent to me that professors essentially report to one another, and then only until they are tenured or promoted to full professor. Arrival at the top rank confers a condition of authority and independence that is unparalleled in basic education. Veteran schoolteachers, no matter how well they are respected, still answer directly to school principals. At the same time, school principals and other school administrators have a degree of authority unparalleled in higher education—traditionally, principals are not responsible to teachers, only for them.

My acculturation to the world of the professor began with exposure to the search committee. The governance structures of public colleges and universities allow for faculty members to be significantly engaged in Human Resources activities; selection committees are generally managed and directed by faculty members. There probably will not be a university administrator present in the room. This is an object lesson in itself: power rests with the committee.

For a professional making the transition to professor, the experience is an opportunity to become accustomed to the idea that faculty members, many of whom do not have a breadth and depth of professional experience comparable to your own, will hold your fate in their hands. You may well be the most experienced person at the table, but the career academics across from you may hold research degrees. Get used to it: a doctorate from a research-intensive university trumps your years of professional experience, and will continue to do so until you gain tenure and are promoted to senior faculty. If you are not a tenure-track faculty member—instructors and lecturers in professional training programs often are not—you may always be regarded as an interloper. It will be assumed by other faculty that your mission is to train professionals, and that theirs is to train scholars.

For me, the second introduction to campus governance came during my first week on the job, when I needed to coordinate the purchase of furniture and equipment for the new school I was to administer. My predecessor, a savvy academician, allowed each faculty member who taught at the school to make her own classroom furniture selection. The orders were written and ready to be signed. My approach was rooted in experience as a public school administrator. I intended to standardize the classroom furniture to allow the greatest future flexibility, and to secure the best price.

I truly had no idea what a sacred cow I was intending to slaughter, but soon learned that it was absolutely necessary, given the culture of the university, to share the decision. I was able to make amends and arrive at a decision with which everyone could live, but I was clearly marked as someone who needed to learn "how things are done around here."

From a school-leadership perspective, this experience of accommodation, and the many others that followed, informed my understanding and teaching of school administration. I continue to be responsible for directing the school, but have largely abandoned principal-centered leadership for a more distributed leadership style. Just as faculty in the school model strong teaching practices, I find that blending traditional public-school administrative approaches with higher-education shared-governance practices leads to a viable and appropriate leadership.

For the professional considering a mid-career or post-career transition to the academic world, time spent with the selection committee is truly the opportunity to sample the academic culture. It is a truism that interviews are two-way processes, and in considering this transition, it is essential that the candidate seek to interview the interviewers. Critical questions will address supports and expectations for meeting the challenge of teaching, expectations of scholarly activity, and expectations of participation in university governance. Clear understanding of these expectations, as well as the regard in which the applicant will be held by traditional professors, can be key to a successful transition from professional to professor.

Phillip F. Diller, EdD
Former director, Grace B. Luhrs Elementary Laboratory School
Associate Professor, Department of Educational Leadership
and Special Education
Shippensburg University of Pennsylvania

CHAPTER 16

De-emphasizing Goodness-of-Fit in the Hiring Process: What Can We Learn from Adoptive Family Adjustment?

By Stephen Saiz

GOODNESS-OF-FIT

The researchers of adoption and adoptive family adjustment have borrowed (adopted) from statistics the term goodness-of-fit (McRoy, Grotevant, and Zurcher 1988). Originally used to describe how well a statistical model fits a certain set of observations, adoption researchers use it to describe how similar the adoptive parents are to the adopted child in terms of appearance, personality, intelligence, or interests. Though the question of goodness-of-fit is losing influence in the adoption process, it was not unusual in previous years to find placement-workers trying to predict the future interests and skills of children adopted at an early age. For instance, if a child's birth parents were Catholic, an effort might be made to place the child with a Catholic family; if the birth parents were athletic, the child might be placed with athletic adoptive parents. This was also known as matching.

It is my experience that when a committee is considering a candidate for an academic position, goodness-of-fit, or matching, of the candidate is often covertly considered. For instance, at our institution we recently had a candidate who had done his doctoral work in the area of corrections. Our campus, in upstate New York, is in close proximity to a number of correctional facilities. Quite reasonably, we on the committee believed that our university would be attractive to the candidate, and the candidate, because of our proximity to prisons, became more attractive to us. That's how goodness-of-fit works.

Some characteristics that might be considered when assessing goodness-of-fit are preferred types of recreation, hobbies, communication style, and research interests. When carefully considered, the list of qualities used to measure goodness-of-fit can become quite long, and it is difficult to determine how much weight these qualities are given in selecting candidates.

I have leaned heavily on the analogy of the adopted family because I believe that adopted families and faculties are constructed in similar fashions and share similar challenges. Here are some of the similarities I have seen.

APPOINTMENT

Faculty members are appointed. The noun "appointment" suggests an arrangement to perform a specific task. It lends a level of specificity and definition to the roles of faculty members, as opposed to more traditional verbs like "hired" or "employed." Similarly, adoptive parents are appointed by the courts to perform very specific tasks. In language reminiscent of a contract, the adoptive parent is appointed by the court "... and the Minor Child shall henceforth be the child of the Petitioners [adoptive parents] for all legal purposes" (State of Alaska 1995). I conducted an informal poll at my institution, asking other faculty why they thought "appointment" was the noun chosen to describe terms of employment. A colleague, the chair of another department, believed it was because the institution wanted to stress the temporariness of the position. Appointments at our institution are for one year, two years, or continuing (i.e., tenured). Similarly, the perceived temporariness of the adoptive placement can, according to Brodzinsky, create anxiety in the adoptee until the ages of twelve, thirteen, or fourteen, for not until that level of cognitive development can the adoptee understand the permanence of the legal relationship (1987).

Furthermore, the appointment of the adoptive family is usually not finalized for twelve or eighteen months. During this time, the adoptive family must behave as a family even while understanding that they are not legally a family until the court decides they are. This post-placement, pre-finalization period can be an anxious time, and can limit the adoptive family's efforts to build attachments: they know in the back of their mind that twelve months from now there may be no family. Similarly, pre-permanent appointment can be an anxious time for junior faculty.

BEWILDERMENT

Despite their assigned roles, the members of adoptive families often report a feeling of bewilderment. The adoptive parents will wonder, "Am I the real parent?" In the literature this is known as a "lack of entitlement," and can lead to an unevenness in nurturing and child-rearing. The reciprocal feeling in adopted children is known as "genealogical bewilderment" (Sants 1964). The adopted child asks, "Who am I? Do I belong here?" In the case of academic appointments, bewilderment among junior faculty typically comes from a feeling of differentness and wondering about their role in their department.

RIVALRY

Sibling rivalry in adoptive families can be intense and debilitating, because adoptees often perceive their place in the family as tenuous. The adoptee is the outsider, the new entity that can often be targeted or scapegoated when the family doesn't work effectively in one way or another (Hartman and Laird 1990; Brodzinsky 1987).

Kenneth Westhues provides in his book *Envy of Excellence* (2006) a list of clues that accompany the exclusionary practices and elimination of higher-education faculty. It is uncanny how similar these clues are to the symptoms seen in families broken by an adoption disruption. Rivalry is a possible factor in both higher education and adoptive families. Perhaps rivalry is inherent in situations in which an individual needs to establish him- or herself in a system that is not ready for change, or not designed to change at all.

PROBLEMS WITH GOODNESS-OF-FIT

Goodness-of-fit has fallen out of favor in the adoption-placement process as international, inter-racial, birth parent-prerogative, special needs, and hard-to-place children in foster care become more prevalent. Placement agencies no longer have the luxury of assessing goodness-of-fit. However, there are more subtle reasons goodness-of-fit no longer holds such sway in adoption placement.

First, we have learned much from the research of attachment. We are learning that children who have a consistent caregiver usually do better than children who experience intermittent or inconsistent care with a relative (Hughes 2000). We have learned that children who are resilient do not become that way thanks to unavailable parents, but to non-related, caring adults, such as scout leaders, coaches, or teachers (Butler 1997).

Second, we have come to understand the necessary deliberateness of constructing an adoptive family (Hartman 1984). When a family is created using goodness-of-fit, there is a likelihood that members will look the same. This can be a concern. If family members look alike, they may not acknowledge their differences and fail to do the work that is necessary to construct an adoptive family. Brodzinsky refers to this failure to recognize differences as a rejection of difference, and cites it as a contributing factor to adoption disruption (1987).

Perhaps goodness-of-fit should begin to hold less sway in the appointment process. There are a number of reasons to de-emphasize it.

SCARCITY OF DOCTORATE-LEVEL CANDIDATES

This has been a growing concern within our regional professional organization, NARACES (North Atlantic Region Association of Counselor Education and Supervision). We are not graduating enough doctoral candidates to fill the positions vacated through retirement and job migration. Committees have been formed in our area to groom master's students for doctoral candidacy. Still, we often have more positions than qualified applicants. I have been on searches in the History Department where they might have fifty doctoral applicants for one temporary appointment, while counselor-education lines have gone unfilled, partly because there has been only a handful of applicants prepared for a tenure-track position.

REDUNDANCY

When goodness-of-fit is applied to a candidate search, it can, I think, lead to a rather homogeneous faculty. Such homogeneity can be injurious. For instance, a counselor-educator is hired because he or she has a certain commitment to school counseling. It is natural for the new counselor to want to teach classes that others with the same commitment choose to teach. That can be a problem, especially if the new hire wants to modify the courses. Such behavior could be looked at as a betrayal: "But when we hired you, we thought you shared our interests and commitments?" If the new hire is effective, he or she may begin to attract a cadre of students with shared interests. It is quite possible that the new hire will be perceived as a threat, which jeopardizes faculty cohesion and communication. Furthermore, if goodness-of-fit is stressed, it may limit the participation of the newly hired professor. Like the adoptive child who becomes the perfect child in order to fit in, the newly hired professor may begin to constrict his or her behavior and contributions in order to avoid friction (Melina 1986).

THE GIFT OF ACKNOWLEDGMENT OF DIFFERENCE

Brodzinsky recognizes the ideal adoptive-family adjustment as acknowledgment of difference (1987). Acknowledgment of difference means the family recognize from the start how different they are from a biologically constructed family. They make an effort to squarely acknowledge their differences and talk about them in an open and encouraging way, a way that celebrates those differences and anticipates the disharmony they may bring.

Recently, while involved in a re-accreditation process at our university, I was asked to contribute to the self-study of our education department. I am an ex-primary-teacher and describe myself as a recovering behaviorist. I once believed in the viability of token economies, check marks on the board, and the shaping of behavior. After my views shifted, I was like a recovering alcoholic who sees only evil in alcohol: I had nothing good to say about behaviorism. I could find a way to blame behaviorism for everything from apathy in our youth to poor oral hygiene. There was a colleague in my working group who saw each of our tasks in the light of behaviorism; it was clear from the beginning that our contradictory modes of describing, assessing, and changing behavior were not a good fit. Nevertheless, we continued to work together. I asked about behaviorism. I inquired as to why he thought it was so useful. I made an effort to understand him beyond a cursory label.

Later we served together on a tenure-review committee. I noticed that his questions, which used to tighten my shoulders and try my patience, began to make sense. I came to see why his students twice recognized him with teaching awards. I am not ready to trade my Adlerian ideas for the ideas of the behaviorists, but I began to believe there was a place for this colleague's questions and considerations. Even so, if he presented himself as a behaviorist in a hiring interview, I would not be eager to hire him, as I would not see him as a good fit with my ideas.

I have come to both understand and believe that my behaviorist colleague's ideas are as important as mine, and that our students need to hear his contribution. In order to facilitate the accreditation process, our dean characterized this acknowledgment of difference as not necessarily an agreement of ideas, but an alignment of purpose. The way I understand it is that we are all in the same boat, so we all have our oars in the water, moving the vessel toward an agreed-on destination. I may be headed there to farm the land, the person next to me may want to get there to start a family, another to study the culture of the inhabitants, another to escape a debt. Regardless, we work together.

I think it will be difficult to de-emphasize goodness-of-fit in the hiring process. To acknowledge and incorporate the differences of others will take dialogue, trust, and acceptance. It is work, difficult work. In the process, I will often need to question the truths that guide my behavior. But in the end, it will be worth it.

By the way, the gentleman who had done doctoral research in corrections and applied to our university was offered the position. Everyone on the committee thought it was an ideal fit. He didn't accept. Perhaps goodness-of-fit, like beauty, is only in the eye of the beholder.

Stephen Saiz, EdD, LPC, LMHC, NCC
Associate Professor and Chair, Department of Counselor Education
State University of New York, Plattsburgh

REFERENCES:

Brodzinsky, David M. 1987. Adjustment to adoption: A psychosocial perspective. *Clinical Psychology Review* 7: 25-47.

Butler, Katy. 1997. The anatomy of resilience. *The Family Therapy Networker* 21 (2): 22-31.

Hartman, Ann. 1984. *Working with adoptive families beyond placement*. New York, NY: Child Welfare League of America.

Hartman, Ann, and Joan Laird. 1990. Family treatment after adoption: Common themes. In *The psychology of adoption*, ed. David M. Brodzinsky and Marshall D. Schechter, 221-239. New York, NY: Oxford University Press.

Hughes, Daniel A. 2000. *Facilitating developmental attachment: The road to emotional recovery and behavior change in foster and adopted children*. New York, NY: Jason Aronson.

Melina, Lois Ruskai. 1986. *Raising adopted children: A manual for adoptive parents*. New York, NY: HarperCollins.

McRoy, Ruth G., Harold D. Grotevant, and Louis A. Zurcher. 1988. *Emotional distur-bance in adopted adolescents: Origins and development*. New York, NY: Praeger.

Sants, H. J. 1964. Genealogical bewilderment in children with substitute parents. *British Journal of Medical Psychology* 37 (2):133-142.

State of Alaska. 1995. Decree of adoption. *Third Superior Court of Alaska,* Case No. 3AN-94-634 P/A.

Westhues, Kenneth. 2006. *The envy of excellence: Administrative mobbing of high-achieving professors*. Illustrated edition. Lewiston, NY: The Edwin Mellen Press, Ltd.

CHAPTER 17

Finding the Fit: The Minutiae of the Academic Job Search

By Amie A. Doughty

What does Cinderella have to do with the academic job search? Can the right job really be like the glass slipper that only fits one person? Perhaps that analogy stretches the reality of the academic job search, but in many ways, it is apt: the person on the search is looking for the right position, just as the department hiring is looking for the right candidate. Credentials and experience matter, of course, but other variables play a more subtle, and often more important, role in the decision to hire someone and, yes, to accept a position.

On my first job search, completed as I finished my dissertation, I chose to apply for any tenure-track position that looked as if it was remotely related to my various skills. I knew that others in my department were more selective with their applications, but I was ready to move on and figured that the worst that could happen was a rejection letter from the school. My initial applications proved quite successful and revealed more clearly than anyone's advice could have that all experience is relevant. Few of the interviews I was offered came about as a result solely of my work in my major area of study—twentieth-century American and Native American literature. Instead, it was my experience in other areas—computer-mediated composition, linguistics, and children's literature particularly—that garnered the most interest from schools, even if the original advertisement claimed to be looking for someone in my major area. The responses also showed me that most schools were looking for unmentioned skills from their candidates; these minutiae cannot be controlled by the candidate, which is why applying to positions that seem marginal is worth the effort.

It is during interviews that the minutiae are revealed. Several of my mentors told me as they helped me prepare for my interviews that the interviews were as much a chance for me to decide if the school was right for me as it was for the schools to decide if I was right for them. I was naturally skeptical of this claim; after all, I was the one coming to them for a job, not the other way around. It was on my second interview that I realized that my mentors had been correct.

At this interview, held at the MLA Conference in Chicago, I went to the designated hotel room and was directed to a seat near a lamp in a corner of the room, wall on one side of me, windows on the other. The interviewers—five men—set up their chairs in a semi-circle around me, between me and the door. As the lone female in the room, I was, to put it mildly, unimpressed with this setup. I became even less impressed as the interview began and the questions revealed that their approach to teaching did not match mine. I was so unhappy with their treatment of me, inadvertent or not, and with the apparent parameters of the position, that I made the decision that I did not want the position—and that I was clearly not right for it in any event. When the group ended the interview with the standard "Do you have any questions for us?" query, I replied by asking about their hockey team (it was a school in Michigan), knowing even as I asked the question that I was throwing the interview.

Before then, I had never expected to be the one deciding against a position—unless I happened to have multiple offers. That single interview showed me that I did have a modicum of control over my search, and subsequent interviews, while still nerve-wracking, were much more comfortable. The experience also emphasized that my instinct to act naturally and be myself was critical in all of these interviews. This advice may sound trite, but, given the artificial nature of the interview, it is extremely important, both during preliminary interviews at a conference and during phone and campus interviews. Schools want to know who candidates really are, to see if candidates fit the particular needs of the department, and candidates should want to know if they will be happy joining the department that interviews them. Without honesty on both sides of the interview— and it does need to go both ways— it is impossible to determine if a job or candidate is right.

Two of my on-campus interviews during my first job search emphasized my lesson from the MLA interview and revealed some of the problems of an on-campus interview. In the first on-campus interview, I was flown to a city about an hour's drive from the university and told to pick up a rental car and drive to the school—something I have since learned is not uncommon for on-campus interviews. Though I did not mind the drive, I was unprepared for the blizzard that arrived with my flight. I was given the option of remaining in the city overnight and being picked up the next day by someone else, but given that this was an interview, I determined to make my way to the university. It was a less-than-hospitable welcome, I thought at the time.

Dinner that night went well, and the next morning began the marathon of meetings. I met with numerous gracious and interesting potential colleagues and thought the interview was progressing well until I was introduced to another faculty member in the hall on the way to a meeting. The faculty member barely acknowledged me, leaving me to feel extremely unwelcome.

Already a bit concerned by some of the information I had learned about the department, and still recovering from the arduous drive through the blizzard, I began to question the suitability of this position. My concern increased after I had dinner with the head of the department: it felt more stilted than normal, and she seemed a bit short with me. Despite these concerns, however, I was hopeful for an offer, because it was late in the spring term and I had yet to receive one. My instinct against the position warred with my desire for employment.

Another campus interview, following shortly on this one, added to my torn desire for a position versus the reality of the position for which I was interviewing. This second interview was a brief—one or two hour—affair. I was picked up at the airport by two members of the department and driven the hour or so to the campus. We got lost twice on the way—not an auspicious start to the interview, which rapidly deteriorated from there. I had to wait several hours for my turn at the interview, but no one thought to provide me with lunch or even directions to a vending machine; following the very brief interview, I was forced to wait yet again for a ride to the airport. Though we did not get lost on the way to the airport, the ride did reveal something about the position that was not mentioned in the interview itself: it carried a teaching load of five courses per semester. Once again I was torn between my desire for employment and my desire to reject the job out of hand, even before the search committee could make a decision.

It wasn't until I had the interview with the university at which I eventually accepted a position that I truly understood how a position could fit a person. My initial interview was via phone with two of the faculty members, and it was as comfortable as a phone interview can be. It was conversational rather than forced, and I knew the interview had gone extremely well even before I received a call the next day inviting me to campus. The campus visit was both exhausting and a joy. I spent four days on campus, meeting the dean, the provost, the entire faculty of the department, and the department's students. The vast majority of the visit was a pleasure (the exception being a meeting with a faculty member whom the entire department had warned me about). Even the April snow felt welcoming because I wasn't driving in it myself. By the time I was driven back to the airport, I knew I had found the right place to work. The reaction of the faculty was equally positive, and it was no surprise to receive an offer from them. It was also a pleasure to accept the offer, after some negotiating. There was no doubt in my mind that this university was the place for me.

And so it was the right fit for six years. Unfortunately, unlike the fairy tale, sometimes the fit changes, and six years after accepting my position at the university, I knew that it was time to move on, no matter how difficult the decision was. This time, however, I had the security of tenure and a previous, successful academic job search, both of which greatly reduced the stress of searching for a new fit. By this time, I had also served on several search committees, and I understood some of the quirks of the job-search process as seen from the searcher's side. I knew more about the underlying qualifications that most jobs require, and was able to target my letters more toward the possible extras I could offer to departments. My experience, which had increased exponentially over six years, also helped make me more marketable.

What was vastly different about this job search, aside from my job security and broader experience, was the type of job I chose to apply for. Rather than apply to all jobs remotely applicable, as I had in my first search, I limited my scope geographically, focusing primarily on the East Coast, where my family lives. My areas of interest had also broadened, so I was able to apply to a greater variety of positions, which led to an interesting array of interviews once the applications were out. Once again, the issue of fit came into play as I learned more about the jobs for which I interviewed. Several positions in particular came across as clearly unsuitable, such as when I interviewed for what had appeared to be an Applied Linguistics job but was, in reality, more a TESOL job; or when what had appeared to be a position in literature and linguistics revealed itself to be a job in composition, with only a small linguistics component.

The true revelation in this job search for me, however, was the interview that never happened. I had been on several campus interviews prior to my interview at SUNY Oneonta, and none of those interviews had gone well enough for me or for the search committees. My interview at SUNY Oneonta once again showed me that it was possible to find a fit. I had spent several days meeting faculty members, students, the dean, and the provost, and knew that I could work comfortably in the environment. My excitement over the possibilities of this position was tempered somewhat by a couple of factors: my last "ideal" job had become far from ideal, and I had another interview scheduled. When the offer came from SUNY Oneonta, I asked them to wait for my decision until my next interview was over, to which they graciously agreed.

Several days before I was scheduled to interview for the other position, I discovered something wrong with it. Until then, the position had looked and sounded ideal. When I decided to do a little more research on the university, I learned that not only were its faculty and administration at odds, but the problems were more severe than those at the university where I was working. No one in the department with which I was interviewing had mentioned this problem; the closest I had come to being told about the problem was a backhand comment by the dean who had invited me to campus. The comment only registered fully when I learned about the problems at the university. It is, of course, understandable that people recruiting new faculty would not want to reveal their problems and deter applicants, but the lack of honesty from the faculty, combined with the situation at my own university, made my decision to cancel the interview and to accept my current position at SUNY Oneonta much easier.

Finding a fit is equally important for the schools searching for new faculty, particularly tenure-track faculty. The search committees on which I have served, and other searches I have been part of via the department, have shown the importance of the minutiae. Most searches start with a general idea of what a department needs most: a generalist, a compositionist, a nineteenth-century British literature scholar, a linguist, a children's literature specialist. This information is front-loaded in the advertisement, and forms the basic requirements for all candidates. Sometimes there will be a second area of equal or near-equal importance. Any combination of specialties is possible, and it is impossible for the applicants to know which of the specialties will take precedence. Following the primary specialties being called for, there will often appear a laundry list of other desirable qualifications. How important is this laundry list? It depends on the department's needs, of course, and even the department itself may not know which of the items on the list will matter most until the applications are read.

When a committee does begin to wade through the applications, the first things the members look at are the basic qualifications. It is easy to eliminate the applicants who don't have the basics, but since the majority do, it becomes necessary to narrow the pool—sometimes over one hundred applicants—to a small set, anywhere from five to fifteen, for preliminary interviews. How is it possible to winnow so many applicants? The laundry list begins to matter, as does the manner in which the applicant presents him- or herself in the letter. The letter of application needs to contain a lot of concrete information. All experiences are relevant, even some that seem unimportant. My first job dealt with my ability to teach linguistics and composition, but it was my experience teaching children's literature—a class that I had taught once while completing my master's degree—that caught the committee's attention. Children's literature wasn't mentioned in the advertisement at all, but I included it both in my letter of application and CV because it was teaching experience I had, and it was noticed.

Applicants cannot know the minutiae that committees are looking for. Sometimes the committee members themselves don't know what the minutiae are until they see an applicant with a skill that resonates. Letters of application that highlight the basic credentials as well as additional skills and experiences are key; the CV and other materials are secondary to the letter in catching the committee's notice. And once the committee has narrowed down the applicant pool, using whatever criteria it has established, the rest of the process is about finding the fit, something that only comes through talking to the applicants. The initial interviews allow the committee members to get a feel for a candidate beyond the applications, to find out from a more personal perspective how the candidate's credentials and, perhaps more importantly, manner mix with the committee. An interview in which there are long silences or other signs of awkwardness may indicate that a candidate (or a job, from the candidate's perspective) is not a good fit. If the initial conversation goes well, be it face-to-face at a conference or in a telephone interview, the next, and real, test of the candidate will be the campus interview.

I have been told by many colleagues, with more search-committee experience than I have, that a candidate can be perfect both in an initial interview and on paper, then absolutely flop during a campus interview. The flopping, in my mind, has more to do with a poor fit than anything else. The campus interview is the real test of a candidate's ability to interact with potential colleagues and students. Most candidates at this point have proven themselves capable of performing the job; the question that search committees and departments are asking is "Can I see myself working with this person for the next thirty years?" Applicants should be asking themselves the same question. The final choice for a position earns a resounding "Yes" in response.

Is there really such a thing as the perfect fit in the job search? Or is the Cinderella analogy ineffective? I believe that there is a job suited to everyone, but it can be difficult to find. I remember telling my friends when I finally accepted my first job that they would know when they found the right one. They didn't believe me until they too had emerged, successful, from the job search. It is possible to find the right fit, both for the person on the job search and for the department searching for a new faculty member. It just takes perseverance and patience.

Amie A. Doughty, PhD
Associate Professor, English
State University of New York, College at Oneonta

CHAPTER 18

Life is a Journey,
Not a Destination:
Trust Your Board of Directors

By Darren E. Dobrinski

I kept in mind two guiding principles while deciding whether to pursue and later secure an academic position. The first was a statement that, at times, may sound cliché: "Life is a journey, not a destination." The second was trusting in the judgment of my "personal board of directors." Following these two guiding principles gave me direction and patience to search for and feel confident in accepting an academic position. My purpose in this narrative is to reflect not only on how I became interested in teaching, but also on how these guiding principles assisted me in my pursuit. I hope that others may benefit from this experience, just as those I teach benefit from my experience as a school psychologist.

In pondering the question of how I came to do what I do today, I reminisced on time spent with graduate colleagues discussing course material, theoretical concepts, interest areas, and future career endeavors. Each colleague's interest had a similarity with some of the future plans represented in the group. Discussions often focused on the here and now of graduate school, from course demands to receiving and providing moral support while completing dissertations. When the discussion turned to our plans for the future, where I am today was not part of my discourse.

Before deciding to enter academia full-time, I worked as a school psychologist for five years in both the public and private sectors. I had the opportunity to practice the many roles and functions of a school psychologist: conducting comprehensive evaluations, providing individual and group counseling, consulting, researching, and contributing to educational services. In that enlightening and demanding position, I was provided countless experiences with children, adolescents, school personnel, and families, to name a few. It is those experiences that have served as an invaluable foundation for teaching graduate students about the field of school psychology.

Academia was not a professional goal for me during graduate school. At that time, I was interested in direct care in the school setting. Nevertheless, I had the opportunity to teach classes as an adjunct faculty member in a school psychology program for three years. This gave me a new perspective on how I could contribute to the field of school psychology. I often received feedback on how helpful it was to have a professor who could provide his own professional examples of the concepts being discussed. It was the feedback from students and faculty that started the evolution of my professional and personal goals. I was realizing that by sharing my experiences as a school psychologist with those studying the same profession, I could help more than those with whom I was working clinically: I could help many other children and families by successfully training and teaching those entering the profession. I found myself delving deeper into the world of academia and, in sharing my passion for the practice of school psychology with future practitioners, was confident I could make a lasting impact on students as they achieved their own professional dreams. Thus, I made the decision to pursue an academic position.

When I truly internalized the thought of being employed full-time as a university professor, I realized I had to make some difficult decisions. I found myself revisiting many of the concepts that I learned while taking a career counseling class during my work toward a master's degree in counseling. I recalled my most influential and inspiring professor saying over and over again: "Life is a journey, not a destination." This simple but profound statement, coming from someone I genuinely liked and respected, provided reassurance and support for my desire to pursue a faculty position. I had already earned my PhD and was a practicing school psychologist. I had a wife and child, and had built a home and a reputation in the city where I lived. Professionally, I had achieved what I set out to achieve. I was at my destination. Life was good.

There was still that feeling, though: the feeling that I could continue to grow and contribute to my profession and make more of an impact on this world. That feeling, and the experience of adjunct teaching, made me wonder if I really was at my destination. The "journey" part of the statement was playing over and over in my mind. If life was a journey, then for me, at this point, it would mean many changes. A journey meant I could lose the familiarity and security of my position, move my family, leave behind friendships, students, and a sense of community, simply because I wanted to continue my professional and personal growth. Journeys are not to be undertaken lightly. This is analogous to the principle suggested by Heifetz where one, in making decisions, needs confidants.

Confidants are those who allow you to put all thoughts, hopes, and doubts in the open. They assist you in sorting them out, in deciding what's in your best interest. It is such confidants to whom I turned: my personal board of directors.

The idea of having a personal board of directors also came from a graduate class. The point of a personal board of directors is having individuals to guide and assist you in making life-altering decisions. My personal board of directors consisted of individuals who have influenced and mentored me both personally and professionally. Some of them were aware that I viewed them as mentors, others may not have been. Some of the directors were mentors in both my personal and professional lives, while others spoke to just one of those roles. In all, there were four.

The president of my board was, and still is, my wife, my strongest advocate in following my pursuit for an academic position, even though it meant that we would have to make many life changes. She, while happy with the living situation we had, was always ready for a new journey; she saw that this change would be positive not only for me, but ultimately for our family. On a professional note, she gave me many suggestions as to what I should ask of those with whom I spoke at various universities, and prepared me for what might be asked of me. We spent many nights after our daughter went to bed discussing whether my current role as a school psychologist was my destination, or if there might be something else to discover.

Our discussions turned from entering academia to entering the hospital and clinical setting. The members of my board who helped me delve deeper into understanding what would be necessary in order to accomplish this type of career change were my in-laws. As they were in the medical field as well as administration, they answered many of my questions and assisted me in meeting with those who were currently practicing. After some time exploring this option, I realized that if I was going to make a change, it would be toward the academic setting, not a different clinical setting. I was already doing the type of clinical work I loved.

Another member of my board was my advisor in graduate school, who provided insightful, practical advice in what to look for in a school psychology program and in a university. I knew I wanted to teach, but was not aware of a university professor's other responsibilities. I had been a teaching adjunct for some time, and knew there were other duties, but did not understand to what extent I would be asked or required to contribute. Two of the duties mentioned were scholarship and service. My advisor described the generalities of each of these duties and emphasized that I should ask the members of the interview committee to talk about these areas specifically, since each university approaches them differently. In addition, she advised me to become familiar with the guidelines for tenure, which is a critical and often overlooked part of pursuing, securing, and maintaining an academic position.

Finally, there was a colleague I will never forget. He had a drive and a purpose from the day he moved from the East Coast to the Midwest. His dedication to success ran from his studies to restoring an abandoned farmhouse to building a boat that ended up floating us down the Missouri—to the chagrin of our wives. It was looking back, remembering the clarity with which he saw his future and the type of professional and personal life he valued, that turned me a bit more towards academia. My personal board of directors provided me the opportunity to talk openly about what I wanted from my career and life. They also gave me guidance and information specific to my new pursuit, or shared their passion and influenced me without even knowing it.

There are over one hundred and fifty educational-specialist, graduate-level programs in school psychology, and approximately fifty doctoral programs in school psychology approved by the National Association of School Psychologists. With this information, as well as the knowledge that there was a shortage of school psychologists, I knew I had a lot of opportunity to pursue an academic position, and was finally ready to do so. In the age of the internet it is not difficult to do a quick search for academic openings; while writing this reflection, halfway through a fall semester, there were sixteen faculty openings listed on the National Association of School Psychologists website. The situation was similar when I started my search for an academic position. As I had already settled into a community and had professional experience, as well as a family, I approached where I was going to apply and what type of position I wanted differently from how others might.

I had my professional standards and goals, and my personal mission statement. I had a career I liked, so I didn't feel the need to take whatever position I was offered. If I was going to make this change, it was going to need to be to a university I believed in and that believed in me. My professional goals were numerous. They included having the ability to teach my own classes in a way I saw fit; the flexibility to create and refine the curriculum to meet current standards of practice; and the resources and time to conduct relevant research in my interest areas, as well as create an on-site clinic that would provide resources to the community while allowing my students frequent clinical experiences. In addition, I required the flexibility of schedule and responsibilities necessary to continue my consulting services. Finally, I had to be assured that what I desired to see happen in the department, university, and community would be supported by my colleagues and administration.

In assessing whether what I desired to see happen would be supported by my colleagues and others, I interviewed the faculty, administrators, students, and community members just as much as, if not more than, they interviewed me. As I mentioned, I had a career and was at a place in life I didn't need to leave. Therefore, if I was to make this change in my, and my family's, life, I felt it important that I pursue a position that I was a made for. In order to be sure that I was pursuing and accepting the best position possible, I had to know the philosophy of the university, its vision and its short- and long-term goals. I also took the time to get to know the community and the available resources, exploring the possibilities of involvement. When I was certain, as much as possible, that the position I now hold was the right one for my professional and personal goals, I accepted the offer of employment.

In looking back at the decisions I have made and experiences I have had, I see a few places and times where I could have stopped and decided that I had reached my destination. However, each time I've continued to stretch and carry on my journey, it has led to something even more fulfilling and unique. I have not regretted the way I came to be a professor of school psychology. The journey up to this point has made me a more effective teacher, and the people who have shared their lives and stories with me are now making an impact on the school psychologists of tomorrow.

There seems to be no wrong path in life, just a variety of paths that lead you, sometimes with detours, to your final destination. Make your decisions with confidence, and realize that if what you decide doesn't end up being your destination, there is always another path to take.

Darren E. Dobrinski, PhD
Associate Professor and School Psychology Clinical Director
Minot State University

CHAPTER 19

Pay Attention to the Details

By Matthew Walker

The academic job search can be exciting and nerve-wracking at the same time. My personal journey in trying to find a position and serving on search committees has taught me a few things that I would like to pass on. There is no magic formula for getting a teaching or staff position, just as there is no perfect job. There are always adjustments and concessions to be made.

Before I go into the different experiences you will have, the best piece of advice I can offer you is to do your research before you apply for any job. Most (if not all) universities and colleges have websites with plenty of information about campus life, the faculty, and the academic curriculum you're interested in. Take advantage of these websites, and let them help you guide your decisions in where you may or may not want to apply.

The very first issue that you will need to examine is your list of preferences. You need to determine what you want to teach, what kind of college you want to work for, and where you want (or are willing) to teach. You will probably know the kind of curriculum you feel most comfortable with, as you'll have lots of experience in a particular area of academe. Using these indices to screen position announcements will make your job-hunting process much less stressful. Depending upon your personal situation, you may have to open up your searches to some secondary locations and college/university selections. However, some people have found that once they work in a certain position for a while, they are much happier than they thought they would be.

It is also important to prepare your application materials carefully. Your vitae is equivalent to a resume in that it reflects your experience in the academic field. The vitae is an opportunity for you to tell the hiring committee about yourself and your professional accomplishments. I suggest that you not add too many items of personal interest, such as your hobbies, family background, or political affiliations. By listing these characteristics, you may inadvertently eliminate yourself from the pool of pre-ferred applicants; for example, if you identify yourself as a Democrat, and the department to which you are applying happens to be made up of Re-publicans. Situations like this are few and far between, but if what you list on your vitae is not related to what you have accomplished as a profes-sional, it is probably best to leave it off. The most important function of the vitae is to show how you will fit in *professionally*. The interview is your opportunity to discover if you feel personally comfortable with your pro-spective colleagues (and vice versa).

Many schools will also want you to provide either a list of professional references or have colleagues or supervisors send in letters of recommen-dation. Either way, I have found that it is best to have current and relevant references or letters. Ask colleagues, supervisors (if you can), or former/current professors for letters or permission to list them as references. It can also help your cause if your references have some connection to the de-partment or university to which you are applying. If one of your current colleagues has, for example, presented a paper with a faculty member from the institution you are applying to, there may be a different perception of that recommendation than one coming from a colleague who knows no one. I would not recommend relying solely on these recommendations to get you the job, but they are important—they have helped the commit-tees I've been on to make sure we were getting the candidate we thought we were. If there is a negative thing said or reported on these letters or in the reference calls, it often sends up a red flag. Your references are not likely to say anything negative; you probably selected them because you hoped they would keep everything positive. Most references won't men-tion anything negative unless directly asked to do so. If they offer any neg-ative points without prompting, the general perception of the committees I have been on is that this negative characteristic is a major problem. The most important things in getting letters of reference or a reference list to-gether are making sure that the people you approach will advocate for you, that you have worked with them or for them recently, and that your expe-riences with them are relevant to the position for which you are applying.

Some schools will also ask for evidence of teaching effectiveness. It is much easier to collect these materials after you have been teaching for a while, but you can certainly compile some good items as a graduate stu-dent. While I was a teaching assistant, I was able to have a few faculty members observe me. They not only provided good, practical advice, but were also able to write official reports that I sent along in many of my application packets. Some schools also offer the opportunity for student feedback. Depending upon the institution you are applying to, they may rate these evaluations as more or less important than peer evaluations, but they are important to include, if you have them. It is also a good idea to submit exercises and activities that you use in your classes. It can provide the committee a preliminary look at your teaching style, as will a statement of teaching philosophy, or explanation of why you teach the way you do. At the very least, a self-reflection on individual lectures/classes can provide a hiring committee with some insight to your teaching behaviors and habits.

Each school will usually list some specific requirements for your application. You may be required to complete an application from the school's Human Resources office. These are typically filed to make sure that the hiring process is fair for all applicants. Many times, the hiring committees will not even see these, or if they do, they simply double-check that what you wrote on the HR forms matches what your wrote on your vitae. You may also be required to send unofficial transcripts to make sure that you have the educational background to teach the courses that you say you can. There is also a legal aspect of this request, as the school wants to determine whether you actually have the degrees you claim you do. Some may say that this is just paranoia or mistrust, but there have been a number of publicized incidents in which people lay false claim to certain degrees.

When compiling these materials, it is important to send everything you can that is listed in the job announcement. If you cannot send something that is listed, you may wish to contact the search chair to see if you might send in something in lieu of the missing item. Don't overcompensate, as it can be just as damaging to send too many materials. I recall an application packet that had as many materials as some tenure and promotion applications! To say the least, this applicant appeared desperate (he even sent what appeared to be a studio photo of himself at his desk). A question you should ask yourself as you are compiling your application materials is, "Does this document provide crucial information that isn't requested, but could help my case for the position?" If the answer is "no," I would suggest not sending it. However, if you answer "yes," you may want to think about sending it along, especially if the document is not lengthy. I applied for a position a number of years ago that did not request evidence of teaching effectiveness (a term widely used in many job advertisements). As a doctoral student who had just finished my dissertation proposal, I had no full-time teaching experience. I had some recent student evaluations and a faculty evaluation, though, and decided to send them. Some time later, after I received the position, I was told that those evaluations made a major difference in that college offering me the position.

Another important item that most colleges and universities require is the application letter. This is a letter that should state a number of important pieces of information that can't be covered in a vitae or other materials. You should mention how you found out about the position, what you are doing now, how you meet the requirements of the position, and why you are applying. In my last letter of application, I let the committee know that, for me, this position would mean being close to a lot of family. This is usually an important factor to mention, as most people want to move and stay close to their families. Most schools want people who will be around for a long time, so let them know why you plan to make this school your last career move (or some other phrase). The letter also functions as a demonstration of your writing style. If it has a lot of errors in spelling and grammar, many people will conclude that you are careless, unintelligent, or both. Be smart: have more than one other person check the letter carefully.

Once you have all of your materials compiled and sent, the wait can be somewhat agonizing. Try to stay positive, as you never know when the phone will ring from a prospective employer. The phone interview may either be a scheduled event or catch you by surprise. I have had both kinds, and prefer for it to be unexpected.

Many schools consider the phone interview a step in the search process, but some do not. Phone interviews are typically meant to screen the upper tier of the applicant pool. If you do get a phone interview, you know you have made the first cut. Most phone interviews involve questions about your experience in teaching; what classes you've taught, and which classes you would prefer to teach; and your experience with students, university service, and research. You may be asked to respond to a few hypothetical situations.

I have a few good pointers for managing these interviews. First, make sure you have a copy of the application materials that you sent to this particular school. This allows you to refer to the very documents they have in front of them. Second, stand up while you are being interviewed. It helps you stay more alert and makes your voice clearer. Finally, keep your answers focused. Don't ramble. You wouldn't like to see the faces the interviewers make while you are going on and on about something that has nothing to do with the question. If the interviewers want more information, they will ask for it. Finally, be polite. It makes a difference.

If the phone interview goes well, you stand a good chance of being asked to come in for a campus interview. If you don't get a campus interview, you may want to call the committee chair (after the search has ended) and ask what you could have done differently to be more successful. Some may respond, others will not. In the end, try not to take it personally. I had a great phone interview with a search-committee chairperson, but did not get a campus interview. After I knew that I wasn't being considered for the position, I asked what I could have done better. She told me to finish my doctoral degree, and I would do fine. It can be something as simple as where you are with your dissertation, or the amount of teaching experience someone else has. The bottom line is to hang in there and keep building your credentials.

If you do get a campus interview, you are in the final round. Some schools may only bring in one candidate, in which case you are in the driver's seat. Other places like to bring in multiple applicants so as to compare them to each other. This is when you need to bring your best. At this stage, the hiring committee is looking for the best fit to the culture of the department and campus. If you have made it this far, congratulate yourself, because you probably beat out many other applicants, some of them quite good.

An important point to remember is that you are interviewing the college or university and the community as much as the search committee is interviewing you. The faculty and administration may fall at your feet, but if the facilities are outdated and the community is not what you thought it would be, you are not obligated to accept an offer of employment. I went to an interview at a large metropolitan college where my academic background matched their teaching needs very well. When I arrived, I was told that most of the classes I would be teaching would be in the evening, and I found that the closest house I could afford would require an hour's commute each way. I left the interview knowing that it just wasn't a good match for me and my family.

The committee will usually have you come in overnight, sometimes for two nights if you are far from the campus. If you are flown in, you will be met at the airport by one or more of the hiring committee, so it is important to look sharp from the moment you get on the plane. Even when you are not being interviewed, the committee is observing you. Dress comfortably, but professionally. A jacket and nice pants usually travel pretty well, without much wrinkling. Once, when I was on a hiring committee for a faculty position, I went to pick up an applicant from the airport. He came off the plane wearing an old, stained t-shirt and old jeans. He did not change his clothes for the evening meal with a few members of the committee. I've since wondered what message he was trying to send with those clothes.

Most on-campus interviews involve a few meals (both casual and formal), meetings with the faculty and an administrator or two, and a sample teaching lesson. Remember that wherever you are, whether it seems formal or not, you are being observed. Never let your guard down. I have heard of a few cases in which candidates go to dinner with a few committee members and run themselves out of contention through their behavior. A colleague of mine told me of a candidate who ordered a number of alcoholic beverages at his dinner with the committee, leaving him quite inebriated and unprofessional. Up to that point, the committee had been very impressed with the candidate. He did not get an offer from that school. Speaking of ordering, stick to something familiar (now is not the time to try escargot or other exotic dishes), and not the most expensive item on the menu. No one wants to feel like you are taking advantage of them, even if it is the school's money.

Visits with the school's faculty are typically closer to an interview, while your time spent with the administration is probably going to be more informative than anything else. I don't remember answering any questions from any administrators, other than what my salary requirements might be and when I would be defending my dissertation. Faculty, on the other hand, will pose more teaching- or research-oriented questions. Most faculty know that you will be somewhat nervous, so you probably won't get any trick questions. Most of the questions will be geared toward what classes you can teach, what your teaching style is, your past teaching experience, your research agenda, and your current research projects. If you can bring some writing samples with you (past articles, lesson plans, current drafts of research articles), do so. You may never show them to anyone, but if asked, you will be ready. I never felt pressured or felt uneasy with any of the questions that faculty asked me. Sometimes they were a bit unexpected, but they were always appropriate. I was once asked who my best student ever was, but that was as unexpected as it ever got for me. Now and then, you may have an old, crusty faculty member try to throw you for a loop, and ask you a question that you aren't supposed to know the answer to, but they just want to see how you think on your feet and how creative you might be. A colleague of mine was asked how many quarters, stacked end to end, it would take to reach the top of the Sears Tower in Chicago. It threw him, but he tried to be as logical and creative as he could. He must have passed that test, because he was offered the position the next week.

A common component of the on-campus interview is the classroom presentation. This is simply a time for you to teach what you've probably taught before, except to a new group of students. The committee primarily wants to see your teaching style and secondarily wants to make sure that you can get up in front of a class and not fall on your face. Schools will either ask you to teach on a certain area or leave the subject up to you. If it is your decision, you should still ask what class you will be coming into, to whom the course is directed (i.e., freshman survey course, or upper-level majors), and what material they are currently covering. If you can, it could be to your advantage to teach material that is related to the current chapter in the course. This shows that you are flexible and versatile, which are two important traits that most committees look for in a potential hire. If you cannot teach the material that is currently being covered, that should not be a big problem. Teach what you know best. I have both been asked to teach on a specific topic (in an area I was comfortable with) and been given the option of choosing my lecture topic. I also have tried to include some sort of activity in the class, not only to help keep things moving, but also to also find out what kind of students I might be teaching the next year. In any case, you may want to inform your contact what you plan to teach about, just to keep things clear. This can help the students you will be speaking to and the professor you are replacing (for that day) to prepare for your lecture.

For the most part, committees look for a long list of positives and focus less on uncovering negatives. I can, however, think of a few instances in which candidates botched their interviews very badly, albeit innocently. One candidate came in to where I was getting a graduate degree and had an interview session with the teaching assistants. She tried to memorize all of our names by singing them along to a popular tune. Ugh. This was clearly a case of someone trying too hard to be funny. Later that night, I was told that the candidate excused herself after finishing her entrée and announced that she would return after she had brushed her teeth. There are some things that are better left unsaid.

Sometimes, what you have in your application materials can work against you. I was the chair of a search committee and received a letter of application from a candidate who revealed a lot more personal information than we needed. It made us question his fit in our department's culture. Hiring committees not only look for a person who can complete the tasks, but also someone who is likable and can fit in.

After you have returned home from the interview, it is customary to send the chair of either the department or the search committee a note of thanks. If you decide that you would like to be taken out of consideration for the position, this is the point at which you should say so. Being courteous and up-front usually prevents any bad feelings from developing. You can simply say that it was not a good fit for you, but if there is something compelling that prevented you from keeping this school as an option, you may wish to share it.

If you are still thinking of the school as a possibility, you are going to be waiting for a phone call—one in which an offer of employment is the main topic of conversation. When it happens, take it in stride. Ask for specifics. Make sure you find out about salary, health benefits, retirement benefits, moving-expenses reimbursement, tuition reduction/waivers if you have a family, personal and sick days, and other benefits. You may also wish to ask about the opportunity to teach summer classes, as it can offer some much-needed supplemental income. This factor played a major part in where I teach now, as the last school I taught at offered very few summer courses.

Most schools will give you at least forty-eight hours to make your decision, but some may give you as much as two weeks. I was tendered an offer by one school, but had an interview scheduled at another. I asked the chair of the search committee to give me an extra week, and he was gracious enough to do so. Other chairs may not choose to provide you that extra time. In the end, I took the first offer. It was a better compensation package than the second college's offer, but that wasn't the only factor in the decision. I respected that the first school gave me the opportunity to take my time, which told me that they valued their employees and wanted to give them opportunities to make good decisions that would be best for everyone.

Negotiating is a very tricky business, but you should have some idea of a few things before you accept the school's first offer. Make sure you have an idea of the cost of living where you are moving, how much you will need to make to maintain your current standard of living, and the housing market in the general vicinity of the college or university. Many people will tell you to always ask for more money than what you are offered. That is your call, and if you are comfortable with it, go ahead. You may need to be ready to deal with negative feelings from either the dean or provost if you ask for 20% more than you are offered. Be reasonable in your request. I have been told by administrators that a request for more than 10% above the initial offer is out of line. A colleague of mine at a private school received the money he initially requested, but didn't receive the raises that others did in the next few years. His request didn't seem too overreaching to him, but to the dean of the college, it must have.

The job search can be an exciting, stressful process. It should not only be a process of finding employment, but also a time for you to find the weaknesses of your professional profile and remedy them. Remember, be yourself during the whole process, because you want the school to hire you, not the person you think they want. Ask others for help and advice in finding your weak points and improving them, and show your best stuff. You will eventually find the place that is best for you; just keep plugging away.

Matthew Walker, PhD
Assistant Professor, Communications
Northwest Missouri State University

CHAPTER 20

Do What You Love

By Richard L. Schwab

Success is not the key to happiness. Happiness is the key to success,
and if you do what you love you will be successful.
— Albert Schweitzer 1875-1965

These words of Albert Schweitzer, one of the world's greatest humanitarians, are important to keep in mind before you make your next career move. Whether it is for a position as a starting assistant professor or a jump from professor to administrator, determining the job that best fits your personal and professional goals takes a substantial investment of time, effort, and thought.

A professorship is the best job in the world—if you find the right fit. A bad match can turn it into the worst job in the world. Hopefully, reading this book and discussing your future with mentors and advisors will assist you in clarifying the type of position that will be compatible with your lifestyle and career goals. As you go through this process, keep in mind that your career will be made not only by the jobs you choose to accept, but by those you turn down. Accordingly, during a job search you are simultaneously trying to convince the employer that you are the right person for the job and trying to ascertain if the job is the right fit for you. To successfully meet both goals, my first suggestion is: invest the same amount of energy in your job search as you did in your graduate studies.

Initially, my career goal was to run an alternative middle school for kids who were not successful in traditional schools. During graduate school, I attended a party that inspired me to reconsider my plan. A faculty member approached me and asked if I had ever considered a career as a professor. I had not, but upon his urging, I sought advice from colleagues, investigated the pros and cons of life in higher education, and thoroughly evaluated my strengths and weaknesses.

This redirection led me to the University of New Hampshire (UNH), where I took a position as a lecturer. Soon after, I became an internal candidate who applied for and obtained a tenure-track job in the education department. In 1990, I left UNH to accept a position as head of the Department of Educational Administration at Drake University in Des Moines, Iowa, a mid-sized private university with a strong history of teaching and outreach. In my second year, I was asked to take on the position of acting dean, and a year later, after a national search, was selected for the deanship. In 1997, I was offered the position of dean at the University of Connecticut's Neag School of Education, and held that position for twelve years until deciding to finish my career doing what I love most, teaching.

During these years, I have chaired or participated in many searches, ranging from law-school dean to men's basketball head coach. Some took place at institutions that value teaching more than research, and some took place at institutions that value research over teaching and service. As dean, I have personally interviewed all finalists for faculty positions and always had the final say in who is hired. At this point in my career, that has involved close to a thousand interviews and the hire of more than three hundred staff and faculty, including endowed chairs and non-tenure-track positions.

My background, especially my experiences at different types of institutions, serves as a lens through which I evaluate and select finalists from the candidate pool. My lens has been colored by watching the careers of those who have soared while others have faltered. It has been affected by my personal philosophy and my experience as both an internal and external candidate for a variety of positions. This undoubtedly holds true for many, if not all, administrators, and is why the advice I share here might differ from others'. Based on the view from where I sit, I have put together suggestions for what a top candidate should take into consideration.

#1. Seek the job you really want

Albert Schweitzer's quote should drive your decisions in the search process. Your decision to pursue a particular position should be based on your answers to the following two questions: "Is the position geared to your strengths?" and "Does the position have the potential for making you happy?"

Choosing a life as a professor means you are comfortable with the fact that, most likely, you will make less money than if you took a position in the private sector or full-time agency work. On the other hand, you will have more freedom and autonomy in deciding how to use your time, you will be surrounded by bright people who will challenge you to think, and you will be paid to be creative! It means you will need to be self-directed and motivated to conduct research, to be an effective teacher, and to be an active participant in the process of faculty governance.

At a Carnegie Research-Intensive university, the emphasis is placed on scholarship, while at a state college or small private school, teaching and service are stressed. Some colleges will require off-campus and online teaching; others will not. One is not better than the other, they're just different. Honesty about your skills and abilities is required to determine the type of culture you will enjoy and flourish in. A thorough investigation on your part is needed to acquire a complete understanding of where the institution places it priorities.

#2. Begin early in building your network

In today's world of instant communication, there is no excuse for not being aware of the range of job opportunities on the market. Proactive applicants read the *Chronicle of Higher Education* online *days* before the openings appear in print. Likewise, advertisements are posted in a variety of professional publications, at annual professional conferences, and at career-services offices. However, my experience has been that the majority of successful candidates are recruited by the search committee through networking.

Success in life is built on strong personal relationships. Nowhere is this more apparent than in the job-search process. The range of people I met through my graduate work has been my main source of support throughout my academic career. My advice to you: begin building your network on the very day you start graduate school. Attend every lecture, seminar, and colloquium you possibly can. Take the time to meet the speakers. Familiarize yourself with their work. Attend national conferences, and in addition to the sessions, be sure to go to receptions hosted by various institutions to meet people. When conducting research, do not be afraid to send notes or emails to authors of articles for the purpose of clarifying information or seeking advice. Scholars who are serious about their work are interested in connecting with others who share their passion and appreciate their work. At some point in your career, such contacts will pay major dividends.

When you are seeking a position, be sure to talk with your key faculty advisors and the professional contacts you have made through your graduate work. They can help you in two ways. First, by providing information and guidance, they can help you shape your view on the type of position that would be a good match for you. Second, when they are aware of your career goals and desired positions, they can become advocates for you, both directly and indirectly. For example, direct connections occur when there are openings at your contacts' own institutions. Indirect connections come into play when your contacts are approached by colleagues soliciting nominations for open positions at other institutions; your contacts are now in a position to put you on those colleagues' radar screens. An advantage of learning about openings in this manner is that you will likely be given the sort of details—about the job or the type of candidate being sought—that aren't included in the advertisement.

I am contacted weekly, through email, letters, and phone calls, by fellow deans who need to fill positions. If a graduate student has worked his or her way onto my radar screen, whether by working on committees, being active in the graduate-student association, or thought-provoking conversations while waiting in line at Starbucks, I make it my job to advocate on his or her behalf. Remember this: deans are judged both by the *quality* of their graduates and *where* those graduates are hired. Helping you is not only the right thing to do; it is in your dean's best interest.

#3. Do some homework before preparing your papers and going to the interview

As assiduously as you should work to identify the right fit from your perspective, remember that the people making the hiring decision will be striving just as diligently to make the right choice. Hiring faculty is one of a dean's most important responsibilities. Think about the implications. First of all, most faculty searches cost the institution more than $50,000. When one calculates the time spent by faculty and administrative staff conducting a search, that figure can reach $100,000. Add to that the start-up costs and expenditures needed to essentially guarantee a three-year contract. The financial investment for an entry-level assistant professor can exceed half a million dollars—not to mention the cost, in human terms, of a bad decision that affects student learning and the productivity of the department. Therefore, a dean is going to do everything in his or her power to select the person with the skills and abilities required to be successful in the position, a person who, the dean believes, will enjoy the work. No dean wants to hire someone who is not going to be a happy, productive faculty member. On the same note, faculty want to hire people who will be good colleagues and elevate the status of their department. So remember, the selection team will invest the time and effort required to ensure it makes a good decision, and you will need to do the same for a position you truly want.

Once you have identified an opening in which you are interested, it is time to do your homework on the department, college, and university. This should be completed *before* preparing the application materials, because the background knowledge you acquire should be skillfully infused throughout those materials. Your personal connections and the web pages of the university, college, and department should serve as your main resources.

Familiarize yourself with departmental programs, the backgrounds of key people, and any strategic planning documents that might be available online. Again, use the network I talked about earlier. It is very likely you will come across the name of a professor whose work you are familiar with or a faculty member who graduated from your alma mater. Maybe it is a connection through your graduate advisor. Don't be afraid to email that person to let him or her know of your interest in a position. Establishing a link can be extremely valuable throughout the process, whether it is discovering information not written in the job description or having a person attend your interview seminar who knows a little more about you than what can be gleaned from the application materials.

#4. Attend to details in preparing your papers

Once you have a clear understanding of the written and unwritten requirements of the position, it is time to prepare your application materials. Every university has a career center, and such centers are helpful in coaching you in assembling your papers. You will receive all kinds of advice on your vitae, from its length to its font style. When searching for a position in higher education, those matters are relatively trivial. What *is* important is the information contained in your vitae and letter of application.

Your vitae provides a comprehensive listing of your professional experiences, and is far more detailed than a resume, which is usually limited to one or two pages. A vitae must be concise, neat, accurate, and supply several methods of contact. Other must-haves include publications, professional presentations, committee work, and a listing of courses you may have taught. Be sure to give yourself credit for any involvement in grant proposals or awards received as a graduate or undergraduate student—if appropriate. Personally, I do not think the length of your vitae is a problem; this is not the business world, in which hundreds of applicants are vying for a position.

You can feel confident that everything you put in your vitae will be reviewed and discussed by many interested faculty, including but not limited to the search committee, the department head, assistant and associate deans, and the dean. Most of them will attend your presentation. At many institutions, the provost will also interview finalists, particularly for tenure-track openings. These people want to assess your potential as a scholar, a teacher, and a team player. It is vital to be factual and not overstate your accomplishments. On more than one occasion, candidates have been dropped because they made seemingly small mistakes, such as listing themselves as second authors of articles when they were third, or indicating that they had papers in press when they were really under review. Generally, those analyzing your credentials believe that if you are not careful in this important endeavor, you will not be attentive to your duties once hired.

The letter of application is even more important than the vitae, in my opinion. Remember, search committees and deans spend a great deal of time developing descriptions for position openings because they often use these descriptions as templates for identifying critical needs and selecting candidates. A vitae only provides a skeleton; your letter fills in the details. It also serves as a good indicator of both your writing abilities and your level of seriousness about the position. We all have our hot buttons in the search process, and mine is the generic letter. It is usually one brief paragraph and goes something like this:

Dear Search Committee,

As you can see from my vitae, my qualifications match your job description. I look forward to having an opportunity to discuss them in the interview.

I read their message this way:

Dear Search Committee,

This job is just another chance for me to hit the send button on my computer. It is your job to figure out how my qualifications and your job description match. Since I am guaranteed an interview, I can tell you how good I am when I meet you. I expect you are smart enough to hire me. If not, your loss.

These applications are easy to eliminate, even if their CVs are strong. Again, the feeling of the search committee, and me in particular, is if the candidate is too lazy to prepare a good cover letter, odds are that he or she is not the type of colleague who will help us accomplish the work that needs to be done.

A good cover letter responds to the key issues identified in the position description. Candidates often work from the job advertisement, but this is a mistake, because they are always abbreviated to save money in advertising. For the vast majority of open positions, the search committee will forward a fully developed description to you. Another option is the school's website, where the full description can often be found. When you have finished writing your cover letter, have a colleague look at it, specifically keeping the description in mind, to see if you addressed the key issues. The more concrete examples of how your experience matches the job requirements, the better. For example, if the job description brings up experience in grant writing, include discussion of any and all roles you have played in grant preparation, even if the work you did was on behalf of the primary investigator. Just make sure that he or she is comfortable talking about your role if contacted.

#5. Prepare your responses to frequently asked questions

Your cover letter and vitae got you through the paper screen, and you are among the finalists to be brought to campus for an interview. This means you have the credentials to obtain the job. You now have two tasks. The first is getting the job offer. The second is gathering information that will help you decide whether you should take the job, should it be offered. Remember the priority level here. Too often I have seen good candidates turn off committees by thinking the job is theirs too soon. The tone of their visit is, "You are lucky to get me" when it should be, "Let's learn more about each other to see if this could be a good fit."

You will have heard advice from others on questions the search committee will ask. My focus is what happens when you meet with the dean or a senior-level administrator who represents the dean. In short, think big picture. Do not assume the dean or administrator will have the same level of knowledge about your background that the committee had. Most often, administrators will be working from information on your vitae and application letter. Unfortunately, you will only have about thirty minutes—maybe an hour—to give a positive impression of yourself and convince this person of your potential for success. No matter how interesting or interested you are, keep in mind that he or she probably has several other meetings that day. Schedules are tight and getting extra time is doubtful.

A dean looks for several things in the interview. First, is the person a good communicator? Interviews are stressful, but the skills needed to handle such situations are the ones you will need to be a successful professor. Simple things like eye contact, body language, and a sense of humor all count in first impressions. Expressing yourself clearly and succinctly is important. If you have thirty minutes with the dean and spend twenty minutes talking about yourself in response to the first question, you have talked too long. Be sure to use your listening skills and answer the questions asked.

A second question the dean will want to have answered is, "Will this person be a good fit for our school or college?" The dean wants to find out that you know something about the college and whether you've thought about the job description. In your responses to his or her questions, keep that in the back of your mind. The more you show that you are seriously competing for the job, the better impression you will make. If possible, share specific examples when making key points.

Finally, the dean wants to determine whether you will accept the offer if it is made. If the qualifications of two candidates are equal, the dean will probably make the offer to the person he or she feels is most likely to accept it. Therefore, the more you assure the dean that you want to join the faculty, the better.

Remember, there are questions the dean cannot ask, particularly about your personal life. Two examples are: "Do we have to worry about finding a job for your spouse or significant other?" and "Do you really want to live in a city and work in an urban campus?"

It is up to you to share what information best communicates your personal circumstances and what factors might or might not influence your decision to take the job when offered. One indirect way to convey that you are likely to join the team is to offer up personal reasons for your interest, in addition to the professional ones. During the interview process, you will be asked several times about why you are interested in the position. Let it be known that you have family or friends in the area, or that you prefer a rural or urban campus (depending on where the college is located). Such statements send subtle messages that you have a special interest in coming, should the job be offered.

The most frequently asked questions from the dean will be something like the following:

1. Can you take a couple of minutes to describe your background and the experiences that have prepared you for this position?

2. What will your research agenda be as a new faculty member?

3. Have you had experience teaching at the university level? What courses do you see yourself teaching here?

4. Why did you choose to apply for this position?

5. What questions do you have for me?

Earlier, I mentioned a few things that can derail an interview. A mistake to be added to that list is failing to convince the dean that you have a realistic understanding of the position. If you are thinking "Duh!", believe me, in a third of the interviews I have conducted, the candidate is unable to articulate *why* the position fits his or her personal and career goals.

Let's take a frequently occurring example of this phenomenon. Emily is a new doctoral graduate who is interviewing for a tenure-track position in curriculum and instruction. In her interview, she talks extensively about how much she enjoys working with elementary school children, how much she enjoys teaching, and how she is really interested in spending the majority of her time in schools working with teachers. Any mention of research or scholarship is an afterthought. At an institution that places its priority on teaching and service, this is an advantage. At a major university where scholarship is emphasized, this will hurt her chances of getting the job. Obtaining tenure is strongly correlated with matching passions to positions.

In my years at a Carnegie Research-Intensive university, watching successful and unsuccessful faculty move up the tenure ladder, I have found that survival in this culture hinges on whether you take joy in writing and in facing the challenges of scholarship. They cannot be viewed as a chore or a rite of passage. On the flip side, if scholarship and research are your passion and teaching is something that you just do as part of the job, stay away from an institution that places a premium on your interactions with students, no matter how geographically appealing the position is. Put simply, Emily becomes a superstar and enjoys her life at one university, but at another, her career never gets off the ground and she is miserable in life. It is better to be happy and productive at a college or university where your skills are appreciated than to be doing work you don't enjoy just to be able to say you are a professor at a top-ranked institution.

Another way candidates can derail an interview with the dean is in how they respond to: "What questions do you have for me?" Responding with questions that show interest in clarifying job expectations are best. The safest questions to ask are those about strategic priorities for the school, promotion and tenure expectations, and how the institution provides support for research and teaching. Save questions about contractual issues for the negotiations phase.

#6. You are not finished when the interview is over

You have finished your interviews and are back on the plane, breathing a sigh of relief that it is all over. Not quite yet! The last step in the process is to show the appropriate amount of interest. While details of the interview are still fresh in your mind, write follow-up thank you notes to the main groups/individuals you had the chance to meet. At this point, it really helps your candidacy if you personalize the note. Share a relevant experience that you may have thought about afterward, or mention something new you learned during the interview. For example, let's say you found out about a new grant that was just awarded in a field where you have expertise or interest. Don't be afraid to share that you are interested in being involved with the project should you be offered the job.

Once you have sent a thank you note, sit tight. Do not pester the search chair unless absolutely necessary or to update your portfolio. The world of higher education moves slowly during the search process. Clearances must be obtained from a range of offices before offers can be made. Being overly anxious could give the impression that you will become a "high maintenance" colleague.

Do what you love

Schweitzer's quote at the beginning of this chapter holds particular meaning for me. I do what I love; otherwise I would have never survived the twelve years as dean at the Neag School. On average, deans spend just three to four years at any one institution. Unfortunately, some find out too late that they don't enjoy certain of the aspects of the job. This limits their ability to succeed and contributes to high levels of stress.

Higher education, whether you are an administrator or faculty member, can be incredibly rewarding. We prepare the next generation of leaders and conduct research that expands our knowledge of important issues. To this day, I am eminently grateful to the professor who recognized I had something to contribute to higher education. I hope some of my advice helps solidify or clarify your search for a new job. My best wishes to all of you who decide that a career in higher education will bring you joy.

Richard L. Schwab, PhD
Raymond Neag Endowed Professor of Educational Leadership
Dean Emeritus, Neag School of Education
The University of Connecticut

CHAPTER 21

Interviewing for Positions in Higher Education: Lessons Learned

By Janelle Cowles

The invitation to interview on campus is a critical step in the process of securing a faculty position. As is true of all steps in this process, there are guidelines for how to conduct oneself during the interview. In higher education this step is, more often than not, interview by ordeal. Candidates invited to campus frequently find that the one to two day interview includes meeting with department faculty, program faculty, department chairs, deans, provosts, and representatives of human services. In addition, candidates are asked to make presentations to faculty and student groups demonstrating teaching skills and communicating their areas of research interest. Moreover, meals are shared with representatives of various groups that have a vital interest in the hiring of new faculty.

As a member of a higher-education faculty, I have experienced the interview ordeal on several occasions. Each experience has contributed to my skills, helping me to create for myself some guidelines that led to my ultimate accomplishment: an interview resulting in a faculty position. Since that time, I have served on several search committees charged with seeking faculty in a number of different academic disciplines. As a member of some committees and the chair of others, I have put my guidelines to the test. Those that proved valid are below.

Guideline #1: Naiveté on display

The first time I accepted an invitation to interview for a position in higher education was shortly after I completed my doctoral degree. A fellow student, former colleague, and friend encouraged me to apply for a position open in her program. She was serving as chair of the search committee and contacted me, urging me to apply. I submitted all the paperwork requirements and survived the telephone interview before being invited to campus. I knew I would need to pack my "interview suit," but dressed quite casually for the flight to the interview destination. I was fortunate that my friend's schedule allowed her to greet my flight. Deplaning, I noticed immediately her professional attire and its stark contrast to my own dress, which didn't even meet the standards of business casual. My interview naiveté became immediately apparent to me. This was not a visit to an old friend. I had not drawn a clear boundary to distinguish my social self from my professional self.

Guideline #2: Say what you know, acknowledge what you don't know

My first interview proved to be an opportunity to learn more than one guideline. During the portion of the interview in which I met with the university's provost, I was asked my beliefs about where in the university's structure the School of Education should be located. Should the School of Education maintain an independent identity as a professional school within itself, or should it merge with the School of Arts and Sciences as a program serving the professional goals of teachers in training? To be honest, I not only didn't understand the philosophical issues involved with this problem, I didn't have enough understanding of university structure to generate a cogent response. However, responding to my perception of this question as a "can you think on your feet?" challenge, I cobbled together what I believed to be a thoughtful answer. Only in retrospect did I recognize that collection of jargon as my attempt to appear more knowledgeable than I was. I learned that if I didn't have enough knowledge or information to respond in a genuinely thoughtful manner, I should acknowledge that.

Guideline #3: Respond with grace

Interviews can and often will deviate from the carefully crafted schedules you will receive prior to arriving on campus. Some changes will challenge your flexibility. I arrived for an interview—dressed in my interview suit—to be met with the announcement that the faculty had decided to invite all candidates to interview on the same days. Our schedules would rotate through the various activities, but our meals would be shared. I was being confronted with the situation of either following or preceding my competition into a meeting or presentation.

I felt torn between responding as an individual and responding as a competitor. I found myself saying, "I wonder what he said" and "I wonder what he did." I struggled to remain focused on what I had to offer to the program, and to avoid responding to my imaginary answers to the questions running through my head. However, anxiety rose to a new intensity as I sat with the other candidates and program faculty during meals. My temptation was to engage in a one-up contest: my teaching experiences are more extensive than yours; my research is more challenging than yours. With an awareness of that temptation and with great effort, I was able to engage in an exchange of experiences and philosophies more professional than competitive. Responding with grace to the unexpected helped me survive this most unexpected turn.

Guideline #4: Acknowledge friendships, cope with enemies

While universities are widely scattered across the nation, the world of higher education can be quite small. Acquaintances with members of various faculties are formed through professional development with fellow students, research partners, attendance at professional conferences, and former instructors. These experiences lead to developing opinions of other professionals. One invitation to interview came from the university where I had earned my master's degree. As a student in that program, I had found myself in the middle of a conflict between two of my professors. My alignment with one developed into a friendship and created an adversarial relationship with the other. Both of these faculty members served on the search committee at the time of my interview.

I found myself dreading my meeting with the professor I had once viewed as my adversary. I expected to encounter questions reflective of old resentments, and was not disappointed. Knowing in advance that I would meet with this faculty member allowed me to prepare myself for an adversarial atmosphere. My goal was to maximize opportunities to reconcile old differences and minimize lingering feelings of resentment.

My meeting with the other former professor posed quite different challenges. I expected to encounter support and respect, and again, I was not disappointed. I also anticipated the possibility of old dynamics being present. My goal was to expand my former professor's attitude of support so that it included respect for my professional development while avoiding a replay of former alignments. If the position were offered to me, both of these faculty members would become my colleagues.

Guideline #5: Be overt with concerns

Faculty in higher education have personal lives. For some, aspects of their personal lives may challenge the mores of faculty or student populations.

The candidate's dilemma centers on how open to be about any aspect of his or her personal life that might pose difficulties with his or her integration into the faculty, should the position be offered and accepted.

I accepted an invitation to interview with a university located in an area that I believed was likely to be socially conservative. I was concerned that aspects of my life would be difficult for the student population to accept, but feared that overtly expressing my concerns would jeopardize my chances of a successful interview. In an effort to covertly explore the prevalence of conservative thought in the university, I stumbled through a series of questions about the political climate of the area. I gained little to assuage my concerns, and I believe I left the impression of being a guarded and defensive person. I learned from this experience to be open with any concerns I might have about how my life would be affected by joining a faculty, which generally entails joining a community. Such openness might cause me to lose the offer, but the faculty would have the information needed to make an informed decision, and I would have the information I needed to make an informed response, should the position be offered.

Guideline #6: Accept an Interview Only if You Would Accept the Position

Bringing a candidate to campus for an interview is a rather large investment of time and money for the university. Search committees devote a great deal of time to reviewing applications in order to identify the few candidates that can reasonably be invited.

I once found myself working in a position that I found satisfying, but was likely to end when its grant-based funding did. I felt an urgency to return to higher education after a brief hiatus. I read position announcements for the descriptions of expectations. I applied for a position that sounded truly consistent with my skills and philosophy. The search committee invited me to campus for an interview. Focusing only on the position, I didn't give consideration to the location of the university in a remote area of the country, far from family. When the position was offered to me, I became acutely aware of its distance from my family. My parents were growing older and their health becoming more frail. I knew that I wanted to be close enough for frequent contact with them. I declined the offer. I learned to consider all the factors involved when deciding whether to accept an invitation to interview.

CONCLUSION

While it sounds as if I attended a great many interviews, I confess to having been through only six, three of which resulted in offers to join a faculty. I hope I have experienced my last interview. When I interviewed for my current position, I approached it in a more informed, less naïve manner. When I encountered questions beyond my ken, I acknowledged my lack of information. I drew on the support of former colleagues and openly explored all concerns about the position, which I knew I would accept if it was offered.

The interview process, as daunting as it can be, is indeed forgiving. Mistakes will be made. Afterward, you will reflect on all the things you would do differently. Knowing that the process can absorb errors, you can go forth on interviews with confidence.

Janelle Cowles, EdD, LPC, RPT-S
Associate Professor and Chair, Counselor Education
The University of Central Missouri

CHAPTER 22

Are You Taking Care of Those Closest to You During the Search?

By Linda McHenry

Take a few moments to reflect on what you truly want to gain from this process. Sure, you want a tenure-track position. Specifically, though, you must determine what you expect to get, what you are willing to lose, and what you hope to negotiate—not just with a search committee, but also with your significant other. If your relationship has managed to sustain itself throughout your studies—courses, exams, paper-writing, general exams, writing a dissertation, revising a dissertation, and defending a dissertation—then you are surely aware of the strains to which relationships can be subjected. You know not only about your field, but also about the inner workings of your relationship. The good news is that you have yet another situation in which you can prove to your beloved that he or she is part of the academic process in which you are invested. The bad news is that you can show your beloved what you are willing to lose in order to pursue and secure your tenure-track position, and that may be him or her.

Before you continue in your process, make sure you are cognizant of the lifestyle you crave, the foods you enjoy eating, the kinds of stores where you prefer to shop, the types of vacations for which you long. Carve out what you must have: what ways you plan for further spiritual development, the type of medical community you will need in your future, the sort of transportation to which you want access. Do this for yourself and for your significant other. Ask your significant other about his or her ideal living situation. Inquire about his or her deal-breakers.

Do this for your own ideal position, and do this for your significant other's ideal position. Understand that your beloved may have career aspirations that require living in some specific part of the country or world. There are those whose job skills can transfer fluidly between fields. There are others whose skills and experiences are specific and do not transfer easily. Assuming your significant other can and will pick up wherever you land is often the first error that begins dismantling a relationship. Make a conscious choice regarding what you are willing to gain and lose regarding your partner.

At this point, you should have a basic understanding of the statistics of graduates receiving job offers in your field. You must also understand the basics in your significant other's field. Go to the career placement office on campus and ask for specifics in both areas. Find out how many in your field were hired, and by whom, in the previous years at your graduating institution. You must, from this point on, understand that even though you are searching for *your* position, there is at least one other person whose life will be affected, whose psyche can be injured, and whose dreams can be broken by the choices you make. That's a lot riding on one job. When you search for a job while in a committed relationship, you are juggling others' lives. Accordingly, you have to exercise some control over a process that may make you feel powerless.

You should see and comment on the predictable ways your partner assists you in job searching. Remember that he or she may scour job advertisements, proofread CVs and cover letters, research particular towns and cities, and cart materials to the post office. These acts of kindness will show you the devotion that your beloved has for both you and your hoped-for position. How are you reciprocating?

It is important to remember that your beloved may not have the same interest or desire as you. Even so, he or she may need to learn the jargon of your field. Trust that he or she is willing to commit to memory key words that produce the most perfect job posting. When your beloved reminds you of your attributes throughout this process, listen to the ways he or she coos your strengths: "Baby, you're the best at constructing arguments about Cubism." This is, after all, part of your love story.

You should expect to one day receive an offer, maybe two. Much will be gained by understanding that your significant other is operating on your behalf—probably more than anyone else, including your dissertation committee. Such validation after the arduous tasks involved in researching, writing, revising, and defending a dissertation seems not only logical, but quite human. It is reasonable to believe that you and your partner have wonderful experiences awaiting you wherever you land. This, the beginning process, is met with enthusiasm and expectation, and co-exists with a true lack of understanding of just how many people are competing with you. If you meet this part of the process with shared enthusiasm and a commitment to sharing in the emotional and time components, you will move quickly to the (hopefully short) phase of rejection.

You and your partner should know from the start that the market is competitive. You doubtless understand that all schools are not the same. One major division is between private and public schools. You cannot assume that a private school does not want anyone who does not abide by its particular creed. There are private schools that understand the importance of diversity within faculty. There are private schools that work to retain a particular faith within the faculty. Before applying to a private school, carefully and thoughtfully read the school's mission statement. Consider how your own beliefs fit within the school's mission. Often you can find mission statements online. Could you pledge your loyalty to this school? If you have any reservations, you should probably move on.

Having carefully selected those jobs that fit best with your skills, talents, and assets, you should narrow your search to schools located in a particular region. Both of you need to be on board in determining the parameters of your map. Urban living has many more career opportunities for significant others. Rural living may prove to be the best fit for those who have recently graduated, as rural schools are sometimes considered teaching schools. At teaching schools, work with students takes precedence over your own research projects. It will be great fun to imagine your lives consisting of sipping cappuccino while walking along a city street, contemplating the intricacies of your field. Fantasies are helpful in relationships in many ways.

You will need to choose how many more letters you can write and send to prospective departments. This is when the paper process shifts to internal dialogue and more discussions with your partner. I believe this stage is crucial to advancing the job-search process. You have to consider whether or not you need to shore up your weaknesses.

Start with your publications. (Really, can you ever have too many?) Pause and consider your evidence of effective teaching. Are your student evaluations solid? Do you have several people attesting to the ways you encourage college students in engaging subject matter? You will have to develop a revised game plan, unique to the field of which you want to become a fully fledged member. You will have to focus on what you have both amassed: wisdom, courage, steadfastness, and a bounty of reasonable letters that can be rewritten. But first, ugly emotions can rear their heads and asses.

It is hard to continue the pursuit of an academic position when most of your friends not in academia are living a financially solvent life. It is damn hard to sit across the table at a restaurant with friends who are ordering appetizers, drinks, and an entrée that costs the postage of a month's worth of applications while you and your sweetheart are splitting an entrée and sipping water. It is difficult to look at cell phone photos from glamorous trips others have taken when you two are barely able to afford your land line, and your last vacation consisted of heading home to stay with relatives for winter break.

You will have to take an honest look at your finances. You will have to tally up any loans you have taken out as a graduate or undergraduate. Use a calculator to establish what payments you will be making. Remember car payments. Then, estimate what kind of rent or mortgage you would like. Again, online research can get you ballpark figures. You will have to consider whether your plans include having a child or more children. You will have to consider your professional goals. Remember that any professional organizations to which you belong as a student will require adjustments for faculty. Through all of this, you will have to remain truthful—not only to yourself, but with your loved one. These are your *bottom dollar* numbers. Before you can realistically continue job searching, you must know how much money you need to earn. Check your student loans. Read the fine print on paying them back. All of them. Sit down with your significant other and discuss what you two must undertake to honor your financial obligations—*both of your financial commitments*.

You must decide, at this point, how you characterize support for each other. Sure, you may be able to waive support one or two times, but after that, you may be dismissed. Like graduate school, job searches can fracture the strongest of unions. While you continue to chase what might feel impossible—landing a tenure-track position—you may do what you believed was equally impossible: fracture your blessed union.

Finally, you will achieve what felt unattainable: you will get a call for an interview. Of course, you will begin to prepare for the litany of possible questions and for your presentation. You will also need to reconcile your financial dreams with your financial reality. To do this, you must consider what kind of dollars you and your significant other will need in order to live in the area of the school. You already know your bottom dollar. Now you have to know whether that figure is sustainable in the area where your interview is taking place. No, you are not putting the cart before the horse. You must determine the likelihood of being able to afford a position. Begin to research online the average salaries of those in the area, using some of the many cost of living calculators available online.

Once at your interview, you or your significant other will need to pick up a local newspaper. Scan the rentals. Some places even list rentals online, although the closer you can get in person, the better the read on the cost of living in that particular area. Resist the temptation to think that your faculty salary will be more than enough. When feasible, you will want to explore possibilities first hand. Check out how much a gallon of milk costs at the local grocery chain. Find out the cost of a cup of coffee. Notice the cost of your meals while there, especially if you eat on campus. Does the university's web page give you any indication of health insurance co-pays? What, for them, constitutes a couple? Married or living together? How much does it cost to cover your family? What kind of co-pay do you have? If you can, find out what the area's public library is like. You can get a feel for the community's attitude toward literacy and education through the number of new books and types of magazines available. Consider the fees for overdue items, as this is a way to get a glimpse into the costs of self-education in the area.

If you have applied for a position with a state school, your significant other can investigate the salaries of professors in the department by checking a book in the school's library. In many cases, he or she will have to show identification and sign the book out, but that works well if your beloved has a different last name. If he or she has your last name, well, nobody is going to think you are nosey for checking out the potential windfall or lack thereof. Do this before you get an offer.

You will need to remember that there is another person who has been waiting to begin this phase of his or her life. The sooner you two openly discuss what your absolute bare bones are for contentment, the sooner you will be able to prepare for furthering your job search. Obviously, you will have to decide what makes your relationship yours. For some, this makes the relationship stronger. Others may have another set of papers to sign: divorce.

There are those couples who remain married while they live in different states. There are those couples whose finances are dire and cannot sustain another year of job searching. There are those couples who continue to have one person rearrange his or her life around the other. And sometimes, there are couples who have fantastic support systems that cover their living and entertainment expenses. Some couples put off beginning their families. Most couples make adjustments.

If and when you do get an offer, you must find the gumption to say, "When will you need my decision?" Pause and repeat the date that you are given. You will need at least a week to crunch your numbers. Do not, I repeat, do not accept the offer minutes after it is made to you. You must now talk to your spouse.

You are not desperate. You do not have to accept just any position you are offered. There are situations in which no offer is better than accepting the only offer. Sure, there are times when any offer would make you feel better, but ponder what it would mean to accept a position in a location where your significant other would have no future in his or her profession. Ponder what it would mean to accept a position where your partner was isolated not only from his or her family, but from any real outlet for his or her creativity. Your significant other has breaking points.

You will also have to know your own breaking points. Geography should have already been discussed. Proximity to airports can be deal breakers as well as deal makers. This is an important discussion to have *before* you receive an offer. Positions exist where it is too expensive to live the kind of lifestyle you have already determined you must have. The key is to know how to recognize that kind.

Your significant other is going to have to make peace with where the position is located. What does the area offer to him or her? Not all college towns are the same. What kinds of things will your beloved have to give up? It might be a good idea to consider the types of things you have given up for him or her, and pass on the list. Or you might want to smile and say, "Please?"

You may reach a moment at which it comes down to deciding what is truly important to you: ending the job search with a life with your beloved in your current area, ending the job search and beginning another career avenue elsewhere, ending the job search and continuing your relationship, or continuing the job search and maintaining your relationship. There really are choices throughout the process. You want to remain cognizant of all of them. And mostly, you want to remain constant with your beloved.

Linda McHenry, MA
Instructor of English Composition
Fort Hays State University

Appendices

Appendix A: Guide to Where to Look 194

Appendix B: Guide to the Type of Position 195

Appendix C: Guide to Benefits 196

Appendix D: Guide to Ancillary Benefits 197

Appendix E: Guide to Location 198

Appendix F: Guide to Accreditation 199

Appendix G: Guide to Technology 200

Appendix H: Guide to Ancillary Departmental/
University Issues 201

Appendix I: Guide to Recommendations 202

Appendix J: Guide to Teaching Artifacts 203

Appendix K: Questions for Faculty Members 204

Appendix L: Questions for Partners/Friends/Family
of Faculty Members 205

Appendix A
Guide to Where to Look

MEDIUM	SOURCE	DAILY	WEEKLY	BI-MONTHLY	MONTHLY
Internet	HigherEdJobs.com				
	chroniclecareers.com				
	listserves				
Journals	(e.g., Hispanic Today)				
Professors	(e.g., Dr. Smith)				
Friends	(e.g., Paul Jones)				

Appendix B
Guide to the Type of Position

	SCHOOL A	SCHOOL B	SCHOOL C	SCHOOL D	SCHOOL E
Teaching*					
Notes					
Scholarly Activities*					
Notes					
Service*					
Notes					
Grants*					
Notes					

*Scale: 1—lowest weight (e.g., teaching 0-1 courses/semester); 7—highest weight (e.g., 4 courses/semester + heavy weight on student evaluations)

Appendix C
Guide to Benefits

SCHOOL		UNIVERSITY A	UNIVERSITY B
School Unionized (Y/N)			
Cost of medical coverage			
	Dependents covered (Y/N)		
	Major medical (Y/N)		
	Co-pay for doctor		
	Deductible		
	Notes		
Cost of prescriptions			
	Co-pay/ prescription		
	Deductible		
	Notes		
Cost of dental			
	Dependents covered (Y/N)		
	Notes		
Cost of vision			
	Dependents covered (Y/N)		
	Notes		

Appendix D
Guide to Ancillary Benefits

SCHOOL	UNIVERSITY A	UNIVERSITY B
Parking		
Sporting events		
Concerts and plays		
Child care		
Dining		

Appendix E
Guide to Location

SCHOOL	UNIVERSITY A	UNIVERSITY B
Geographic location		
Urban, suburban, rural		
Cost of living		
Commute time		
Distance to family		
Area activities		

Appendix F
Guide to Accreditation

	UNIVERSITY-WIDE (E.G., MIDDLE STATES)		COLLEGE (E.G., NCATE)		DEPARTMENT (E.G., CACREP)	
University A	Yes	No	Yes	No	Yes	No
University B	Yes	No	Yes	No	Yes	No
University C	Yes	No	Yes	No	Yes	No
University D	Yes	No	Yes	No	Yes	No
University E	Yes	No	Yes	No	Yes	No
University F	Yes	No	Yes	No	Yes	No
University G	Yes	No	Yes	No	Yes	No

Appendix G
Guide to Technology

	DISTANCE EDUCATION (e.g., video-conferencing technologies for the classroom)		COURSE AUGMENTATION TECHNOLGIES (e.g., BlackBoard)		CLASSROOM TECHNOLOGIES (e.g., computers in the classroom, smart carts, video-projectors)	
University A	Yes	No	Yes	No	Yes	No
Notes						
University B	Yes	No	Yes	No	Yes	No
Notes						
University C	Yes	No	Yes	No	Yes	No
Notes						
University D	Yes	No	Yes	No	Yes	No
Notes						
University E	Yes	No	Yes	No	Yes	No
Notes						
University F	Yes	No	Yes	No	Yes	No
Notes						

Appendix **H**
Guide to Ancillary Departmental/University Issues

	UNIVERSITY A	UNIVERSITY B
Size of department		
Responsibilites & duties		
Position you are filling		
Financial position of university		
Funding for conferences, etc.		

Appendix 1
Guide to Recommendations

	DR. JONES	DR. RENEE	DR. HELSEL	DR. SEDONA	DR. COUSER
Teaching					
Research					
Service					
Presentations					
Collegiality					
Grant-writing					
Technology					
Diversity					
Community service					
Leadership					
Other					

Appendix J
Guide to Teaching Artifacts

	STUDENT EVALUATIONS (Overall effectivenss)	OBSERVATION LETTERS	STUDENT COMMENTS	TECHNOLOGY USED
Course A				
Course B				
Course C				
Course D				
Course E				

Appendex K
Questions for Faculty Members

On a scale of 1-10 (10 being the highest level of stress; 1, the lowest), what level of stress did you experience during the search?

What specific coping methods did you employ during the search?

What was the most surprising thing you experienced during your search for an academic position?

What were some of the most effective strategies you incorporated into your search?

What were some of the activities that proved either ineffective or counterproductive for you during the search?

What advice would you give to individuals seeking academic positions?

What were the key methods you utilized to get information about available positions?

What advice can you share with applicants about building a strong packet that represents them well?

How can an applicant prepare for the phone and campus interviews?

What do you feel was the most significant positive action you took during the negotiation process?

If you have served on a hiring committee, what did an applicant do that made him or her stand out from a highly-qualified, competitive group of fellow applicants?

Appendix L
Questions for Partners/Friends/ Family
of Faculty Members

On a scale of 1-10 (10 being the highest level of stress; 1, the lowest), what level of stress did you experience during the search?

What was the most surprising thing you experienced during the actual job search?

What were some of the ways you were able to positively and effectively aid your partner/friend/family member in his/her search?

What were some of the behaviors that proved either ineffective or counterproductive during the search?

What advice would you give to individuals seeking academic positions?

What were some of the requirements you had as your significant other/family member/friend conducted the search?

In hindsight, is there anything you wished you knew prior to your partner/friend/family member embarking on the job search?

List of Annotated References and Useful Resources for the Job Searcher

ONLINE

About.com: Graduate School: http://gradschool.about.com/od/getanacademicjob/Secure_an_Academic_Position.htm

Practical advice for searchers, ranging from locating positions to writing your vitae. Loads of pragmatic papers written to help guide you through the process.

Academic Careers Online: http://www.academiccareers.com/

Postings of academic jobs in many disciplines; also offers services for applicants wanting to have their information shared with search committees. The postings cover teaching, research, and administrative positions.

Academic Keys: http://academickeys.com/

Information about the job search and many listings of jobs in various disciplines.

American Association of Community Colleges: http://www2.aacc.nche.edu/research/index.htm

Information for applicants looking for positions in community colleges; also provides articles related to the job search.

American Association of University Professors: http://www.aaup.org/AAUP/career/

Strategically useful information for job searching in academia. Provides searchers with listings of job openings, as well as resources for posting your information for others to view.

American Mathematical Association: http://www.ams.org/eims/

Offers searchers in the field of mathematics both a place to search job listings specific to their field and to host their materials (vitae, cover letter).

Association of Jesuit Colleges & Universities: http://office.ajcunet.edu/jobbank/

Provides users with a job bank for position openings in Jesuit institutions of higher education.

Computer Science Faculty Job-Search Resources: http://www.cis.upenn.edu/~sweirich/resources.htm

Provides resources and information particular to job searches in computer science. Articles and information about this field are linked to the site, as well as stories from the field.

Council for Christian Colleges & Universities: http://www.cccu.org/careers

Provides applicants with information, job listings, and tips for those individuals looking for postings at Christian-based institutions.

Educause: http://www.educause.edu/content.asp?page_id=38&bhcp=1

Lists job openings in the information technology field.

HigherEdJobs.com: http://www.higheredjobs.com/

Offers many postings of job openings across the country. Users can also post their vitae and contact information for others to view.

Hispanic Outlook in Higher Education: http://www.hispanicoutlook.com/listings.htm

Lists positions in many fields in higher education.

HNet: http://www.h-net.org/jobs/

Posts openings in humanities and social sciences.

IMDiversity.com: http://www.iminorities.com/

Offers job lists and information about the academic job search. Provides support and suggestions for minority-culture members regarding the search, advice on finding diversity-sensitive employers, and a place to post materials.

National Institutes for Health: http://www.training.nih.gov/careers/careercenter/advice.html

Advice for applicants looking in the field of health services. Provides links to websites with job postings in health services, as well as information on conducting a dual search (academic and non-academic job searches).

Preparing future faculty: http://www.preparing-faculty.org/PFFWeb.Resources.htm

Useful tips on teaching, research, and job searching in academia. Has information useful for new faculty, such as the role of faculty, developing and maintaining partnerships, and effective mentoring.

The Academic Job Search . . . Making Effective Impressions: http://www1.umn.edu/ohr/teachlearn/tutorials/jobsearch/index.html.

Specific information on writing your vitae, cover letters, and other necessary materials. Also has useful information on interviewing and finding the right institutional fit.

The Academic Job Search: http://www.english.uga.edu/gradeng/jobs/academic.html

Practical and useful; targets applicants in English. Links to other searchable websites, offers practical advice to those in the field of English, and has suggestions for writing for publication.

The Academic Position Network: http://www.apnjobs.com/

Job openings in many different fields of study.

The Adjunct Advocate: http://www.adjunctnation.com/jobs

Tips and listings for finding an adjunct position. Also offers a place for users to post their vitae and cover letter to be viewed by institutions looking for adjunct faculty.

The *Chronicle of Higher Education*: http://chronicle.com/jobs/

Tips, strategies, editorials, and valuable insights into the academic job search. An extensive up-to-date listing of position openings in many academic fields. Users can post their materials for others to view and search.

The Higher Education Resource Hub: http://www.higher-ed.org/jobs.html

Many links to websites that list job openings, as well as sites that provide advice to searchers.

Universityjobs.com: http://www.universityjobs.com/

Lists many academic positions and provides a place to post your vitae and cover letter.

PRINT

Arnold, Danny R. 2009. *147 Publishing tips for professors*. Madison, WI: Atwood Publishing. Straight-forward and thoughtful advice on publishing, written specifically for professors. Author Danny Arnold offers practical considerations about everything from finding the best-fit publication for your writing, to rethinking your research and teaching, to planning for presentations.

Forno, Dawn M., and Cheryl Reed. 1999. *Job search in academe: Strategic rhetorics for faculty job candidates*. Sterling, VA: Stylus. Information and suggestions on conducting a successful job search. The authors target a broad audience of fields and provide useful information for searchers looking for positions that range from adjunct to visiting to assistant professor.

Hume, Kathryn. 2004. *Surviving your academic job hunt: Advice for humanities PhDs*. New York, NY: Palgrave Macmillan. Focuses on information for searchers in the field of humanities. Provides information on the job search in academia and for assistant professors in the humanities.

Barnes, Sandra L. 2007. *On the market: Strategies for a successful academic job search*. Boulder, CO: Lynne Reinner. Targets social sciences and humanities and covers many aspects of the academic job search.

Heiberger, Mary Morris and Julia Miller Vick. 2001. *The academic job search handbook (3rd edition)*. Philadelphia, PA: University of Pennsylvania Press. Information on planning and conducting your search, and what to do after you have started your career and are working toward tenure and promotion.

Goldsmith, John A., John Komlos, and Penny Schine Gold. 2001. *The Chicago guide to your academic career: A portable mentor for scholars from graduate school through tenure*. Chicago, IL: University of Chicago Press. Guides the reader from the decision to become a faculty member to securing an academic position to navigating the position itself. Special attention is paid to the life of an assistant professor in academia.

Schoenfeld, A. Clay, and Robert Magnan. 2004. *Mentor in a manual: Climbing the academic ladder to tenure (3rd edition)*. Madison, WI: Atwood Publishing. Guides the reader through the path to tenure, using an example school and assistant professor. The authors provide valuable and thorough counsel on this important element of the academic career.

Index

A

academia 104, 133, 138
  transitioning to 133 - 135, 154 - 155
academic ranks 25
accreditation 30, *31*, 106
administrators, meeting with 60, 128, 175 - 178
ancillary benefits 27, *29*, 34
application letter
  See cover letter
application packet 35 - 49, 75 - 76, 110, 124 - 126, 159 - 162
  additional materials 161
  personal information, divulging 20 - 21, 159 - 160, 165 - 166
  tailoring to posting 18 - 19, 35, 101, 119
application process 43, 45 - 46, 49, 124 - 126, 133, 159 - 162
  following up 46, 49
  preparation 173, 189
  researching institution 104, 159, 173
  See also search process

B

benefits 27 - 28

C

campus interview
  See campus visit
campus visit 17, 56 - 68, 112 - 113, 119, 127 - 130, 146 - 147, 163 - 164, 181

administrators, meeting with 60, 112, 128, 164, 175 - 178
  dean, meeting with 59 - 60, 175 - 178
  department chair, meeting with 63
  faculty, meeting with 128, 164
  follow up 67 - 68, 81, 120, 166, 178
  Group meeting 129 - 130
  meals 58 - 59, 128 - 130, 164
  preparation 16, 128, 164
  research presentation 61 - 62, 112 - 113, 129
  schedule 57, 128
  search committee, interview with 64 - 65, 80 - 81, 112, 130
  teaching presentation 40, 63, 129, 165
Carnegie Foundation for the Advancement of Teaching 105
certification 34
Chronicle of Higher Education 86, 117, 131, 171
chroniclecareers.com 23, 49
classroom presentation
  See teaching presentation
collective bargaining 26 - 27, 33, 69
conferences 16, 34, 42, 110, 171
  networking and 52 - 53
cost of living 92 - 93, 96, 166, 190 - 191
cover letter 42 - 45, 76 - 77, 110 - 111, 162, 174
  contents 43, 110, 150
  tailoring to posting 45, 110, 174 - 175
culture, community 28, 100, 105, 114

culture, institution 100, 104 - 105, 116, 134 - 135, 157, 189

D

dean, meeting with 59 - 60, 175 - 178

discrimination 19, 100

distance education 31, 171

diversity 19 - 21, 100 - 102, 183 - 184
  fit and 140 - 142
  hiring process and 19 - 20

E

exit interview 67

F

financial commitments 189 - 190

financial health of, institution 32 - 33

fit 13, 49, 56, 59, 103 - 104, 115 - 117, 145 - 151, 160, 169
  adoption process, similarities to 137-140
  culture, community 92, 105, 163, 184
  culture, institution 99, 116 - 117, 146 - 147, 149, 189
  de-emphasizing 140 - 142
  diversity and 100, 184
  establishing 103 - 107
  interview and 55, 146, 150, 175
  needs, applicant 31, 106, 116, 156 - 157, 163, 166, 170 - 171, 173, 189
  needs, institution 104, 111, 146, 150, 172, 176 - 177
  research agenda and 41, 62

G

geographic location 25, 27, *29*, 99, 189, 192

goodness-of-fit
  See fit

grant-writing 24 - 25, 91

H

Higher Education Directory 116

HigherEdJobs.com 23, 49, 117

hiring committee
  See search committee

hiring process

See selection process

I

internal candidate 83 - 84, 118

interview 17, 59 - 60, 63, 119 - 120, 130, 135, 146, 175 - 178, 181 - 185
  assessing fit 145 - 146, 150, 175
  exit interview 67
  phone interview 55 - 56, 78 - 79, 127, 162
  preparation 79 - 80, 119, 127
  questions, interviewee 30, 56, 65 - 66, 104 - 105, 112, 127, 130, 178
  questions, interviewer 64, 66 - 67, 102, 162, 164 - 165, 175 - 177
  strategies 64, 79 - 80, 112, 162 - 163, 181 - 184
  See also campus visit

J

job offer 69 - 70, 130, 166
  negotiation and 69, 113 - 114, 130, 166 - 167
  refusing 166

job posting 13, 49, *50*
  finding, resources for 17 - 18, 23, *24*, 49, 117, 131, 156
  origins 31 - 33
  unlisted responsibilities 30, 101, 147, 173

L

letters of recommendation 35 - 36, *37*, 110 - 111, 126
  See also references

M

mentor 18, 63, 65, 118, 124, 145 - 146, 155 - 156, 169

methodological expertise 41 - 42

N

negotiation process 69 - 72, 113, 166 - 167

networking 18, 50 - 53, 110, 171 - 172

P

personal board of directors
  See support network
phone interview 55 - 56, 78 - 79, 127, 162
position 23-32, 82 - 83
  listings 17 - 18, 23, *24*, 49, 117
  origins 31 - 33
  preferences, applicant 14, 27 - 30, 156-157, 159
  requirements 24 - 25, 30, 49 - 50, 101, 173
  types 24 - 25, *26*, 89 - 91, 116, 171
presentations 25, 42, 52 - 53
private institutions 82, 171, 189
professional goals 13, 92 - 93, 105, 154, 156, 169 - 170, 187
professional network 18, 29, 40, 50 - 53, 172, 183
professional organizations 34, 110, 131, 140, 156, 190
professional writing 16, 25, 40 - 41, 109, 116, 124
promotion 25, 29, 117, 121
public institutions 171, 189

Q

quality of life 28, 92 - 93, 96, 114, 187, 192

R

references 36, 119 - 120
  See also letters of recommendation
rejection 81 - 82, 87, 112, 118 - 119, 123
  following up 163
research agenda 41 - 42, 110 - 111, 116, 120, 125 - 126, 164
research presentation 61 - 62, 112 - 113, 129
research seminar
  See research presentation
Research track 89 - 94
  search strategies 90 - 91

S

salary 25 - 27
  negotiation and 26 - 27, 69, 166 - 167
  ranges 26
scholarship 24 - 25, 109
search committee 16, 30, 35, 41 - 42, 45, 134
  evaluation form 45, 49 - 50, *51-52*
  interview with 64 - 65, 80 - 81, 112, 130
search process 13 - 17, 123 - 131
  emotional toll 15 - 17, 190
  job posting, finding 23, *24*
  maintaining relationship during 187 - 192
  preparation 14, 19, 109 - 110, 123, 159
  researching institution 29 - 30, 32 - 33, 79, 116 - 117, 159
  timeline 15 - 19, *44*
  unfavorable market and 85 - 88
selection process 43, 45, 49 - 50, 117 - 118, 126 - 130, 133
  bias and 117 - 118
  diversity and 19 - 21
  eliminating candidates 46, 126 - 127, 150, 165 - 166, 174, 177
  evaluation form 49-50, *51-52*
  timeline 15 - 17, 118
  unmentioned skills 145, 150
  See also interview
  See also search committee
self-assessment 106, 115 - 116, 123, 159, 189
service 24 - 25, 42
significant other 92, 187 - 192
  See also support network
single parenting 95 - 97
spouse
  See significant other
support network 15, 153, 155 - 156, 188
  See also signifigant other

T

teaching 97, 111, 116
  load 24, 70, 116
  style 31, 164
  technology and 31 - 32, 70
teaching artifacts 37 - 38, 120, 160 - 162
  See also teaching portfolio
teaching demonstration
  See teaching presentation
teaching philosophy 38 - 41, *39*, 111, 125, 146
teaching portfolio 38 - 40
  See also teaching artifacts
teaching presentation 40, 63, 100, 129, 165
  preparation 165
technology 30 - *32*, 129
tenure 25, 29, 89 - 90, 117, 121
tenure track 85, 89 - 91, 93, 96
thank you notes 67 - 68, 81, 166, 178

U

unfavorable market 85 - 86
  search strategies 86 - 88
union 27, 33, 69

V

vitae 18, 30, 42, 45 - 46, *47 - 48*, 77 - 78, 110, 119, 125, 159 - 160, 173 - 174
  contents 77 - 78, 173 - 174
  personal interests 160
  tailoring to posting 45

About the Authors

BILL MCHENRY, PhD, LPC, NCC is an associate professor of Counseling and Psychology at Texas A&M University-Texarkana. His doctorate is in Counselor Education from the University of South Dakota. He has been a member of multiple search committees (8 for faculty positions, 3 for administrative positions). Bill has taught career development courses at the graduate level and conducted numerous career development workshops. Bill and his wife, Melissa, have four children—Meghan, Billy, Katie, and Shane.

S. KENT BUTLER, JR., PhD, LPC, NCC, NCSC is an associate professor at the University of Central Florida. He holds a PhD in Educational Psychology, with a concentration in Counseling Psychology, from the University of Connecticut. Dr. Butler has diverse experiences in counseling and teaching from the states of Connecticut, Texas, and Missouri. While at the University of Missouri–St. Louis, Dr. Butler was the Chair of the Division of Counseling and Family Therapy's Review Board, Director of the Division's Counseling Center, and Coordinator of the School Counseling Program. He continues to work closely with colleagues, students, and clients surrounding issues of diversity and social justice in counseling.

JIM MCHENRY, Ed.D., LPC, NCC, CRC, is Professor Emeritus, Edinboro University of Pennsylvania. He taught thirty-two years in the Department of Counseling and Human development. Jim also served in a number of on-campus counseling and administrative roles with students with disabilities and students who were economically or academically disadvantaged. He has served on numerous search committees both within and external to the Department. Jim taught career decision-making and career development courses at both the graduate and undergraduate level.